Lederer
on
Language

Also by Richard Lederer

Adventures of a Verbivore
Amazing Words
American Trivia (with Caroline McCullagh)
Anguished English
Animal Crackers Junior (with Jim Ertner)
The Ants Are My Friends (with Stan Kegel)
Basic Verbal Skills (with Philip Burnham)
The Big Book of Word Play Crosswords (with Gayle Dean)
The Bride of Anguished English
Building Bridge (with Bo Schambelan and Arnold Fisher)
The Circus of Words
Classic Literary Trivia
Cleverly Comical Animal Jokes (with Jim Ertner)
Comma Sense (with John Shore)
Crazy English
The Cunning Linguist
Fractured English
Get Thee to a Punnery
The Giant Book of Animal Jokes (with Jim Ertner)
The Gift of Age
Have Yourself a Punny Little Christmas
Hilarious Holiday Humor (with Stan Kegel)
Literary Trivia
A Man of My Words
The Miracle of Language
More Anguished English
The Play of Words
Presidential Trivia
Pun & Games
Puns Spooken Here
The Revenge of Anguished English
Rip Roaring Animal Jokes (with Jim Ertner)
Sleeping Dogs Don't Lay (with Richard Dowis)
Super Funny Animal Jokes (with Jim Ertner)
A Treasury for Cat Lovers
A Treasury for Dog Lovers
Wild & Wacky Animal Jokes (with Jim Ertner)
The Word Circus
Word Wizard
The Write Way (with Richard Dowis)

merry Christmas 2016
to Dennis,
my fellow verbivore,

Lederer
on
Language

**A Celebration
of English,
Good Grammar,
and Wordplay**

Richard Lederer

RICHARD LEDERER

Marion Street Press

Portland, Oregon

To Frederic Cassidy, Joan Houston Hall, and their many colleagues,
on completing, after fifty years,
the *Dictionary of American Regional English*

Acknowledgments

Thanks to Charles Harrington Elster for his hand in shaping "A Declaration of Language Independence" and to Barbara Berti for permission to use excerpts from my appearance on *The Jim Bohannon Show*.

Versions of "Stamp Out Fadspeak" and "How Wise is Proverbial Wisdom" first appeared in *Verbatim* and "A Declaration of Language Independence" in my foreword to *Dictionary of Americanisms* (John Wiley & Sons, 2003).

Portions of this book first appeared in *A Man of My Words* (St. Martin's, 2003).

Published by Marion Street Press
4207 SE Woodstock Blvd # 168
Portland, OR 97206-6267
USA
http://www.marionstreetpress.com/

Orders and review copies: (800) 888-4741

Printed in the United States of America
ISBN 978-1-936863-13-6

Cover design by Adam Graniss (Rockchild Designs)
Front cover photo by Hoffman Photographic
Back cover photo by Kim Treffinger

Library of Congress Cataloging-in-Publication Data pending

Contents

Acknowledgments / *ii*
Introduction: Confessions of a Verbivore / *vii*

A CELEBRATION OF ENGLISH
Our Abounding English Language / 2
Doing a Number on English / 4
A Guide to Britspeak, A to Zed / 8

THIS AMERICAN LANGUAGE
A Declaration of Language Independence / 14
Talking Turkey / 17
All-American Dialects / 20
Slang As It Is Slung / 25
A Circus of Words / 28
Words from Our Presidents / 30
Stamp Out Fadspeak! / 33
Like, What's Happening to Our Language? / 36

THE GLAMOUR OF GRAMMAR
Conan the Grammarian / 40
Laying Down the Law—Without Lying Down on the Job / 47
Sex and the Singular Pronoun / 49
An Open Letter to Ann Landers / 51

SPELLBOUND
Under a Spell / 56
I Before *E,* Except? . . . / 62
Fairly Familiar Phrases / 65

GETTING THE WORD OUT
Writing Is . . . / 68
How I Write / 69
Plane Talk / 72
Radio Days / 75
English with a Russian Dressing / 82

THE COLLIDE-O-SCOPE OF LANGUAGE
How Wise Is Proverbial Wisdom? / 88
Words That Never Stray / 92
Heads Without Tails / 96
Our Uppity English Language / 98
On Palindromes / 100
The Long and the Short of English / 103

THE ROMANCE OF WORDS
Toothsome Etymologies / 108
Haunted Words / 112
My Kids the Poker Players / 117
On Paradox / 121
A Primer of Political Words / 123
The True Meanings of Christmas / 127
Literature Lives! / 131

IT'S A PUNDERFUL LIFE
Jest for the Pun of It / 136
Pun Your Way to Success / 140
Nothing Works for Me / 144
A Bilingual Pun is Twice the Fun / 147
My Favorite Monsters / 151

Answers to Quizzes and Games / 154

Introduction: Confessions of a Verbivore

One day I found myself chatting with Marilyn Frazier's class of sixth-grade students at Broken Ground School in Concord, New Hampshire, about the joys of language and the challenges of the writing life. During the question-and-answer session that followed, one of the boys in the class asked me, "Dr. Lederer, where do you get your ideas for your books?"

Ever since I became a writer, I had found that question to be the most difficult to answer and had only recently come up with an analogy that I thought would satisfy both my audience and me. Pouncing on the opportunity to unveil my spanking new explanation for the first time, I countered with "Where does the spider get its web?"

The idea, of course, was that the spider is not aware of how it spins out intricate and beautiful patterns with the silky material that is simply a natural part of itself. Asking a writer to account for the genesis of his or her ideas is as futile as asking a spider to explain the source of its web and the method of its construction.

So when the young man asked his question, I replied, "Where does the spider get its web?"

He shot right back, "From its butt!"

Since that visit, I've checked out the boy's assertion, and, sure enough, spiders do produce their silk in glands located in their posteriors. The glands open through the tiny spinnerets located at the hind end of the abdomen. Well, it may be that for lo these many years I've been talking and writing through my butt, but that doesn't stop me from being a self-confessed and unrepentant verbivore.

Carnivores eat flesh and meat; piscivores eat fish; herbivores consume plants and vegetables; verbivores devour words. I am such a creature. My whole life I have feasted on words—ogled their appetizing shapes, colors, and textures; swished them around in my mouth; lingered over their many tastes; felt their juices run down my chin. During my adventures as a fly-by-the-roof-of-the-mouth, user-friendly wizard of idiom, I have met thousands of other wordaholics, logolepts, and verbivores, folks who also eat their words.

What is there about words that makes a language person love them so? The answers are probably as varied as the number of verbivores themselves. There are as many reasons to love words as there are people who love them. How do we love thee, language? Let us count the ways.

Some word people are intrigued by the birth and life of words. They become enthusiastic, ebullient, and enchanted when they discover that *enthusiastic* literally means "possessed by a god"; *ebullient* "boiling over, spouting out"; and *enchanted* "singing a magic song." They are rendered starry-eyed by the insight that *disaster (dis-aster)* literally means "ill-starred" and intoxicated by the information that *intoxicated* has poison in its heart. They love the fact that *amateur* is cobbled from the very first verb that all students of Latin learn— *amo:* "I love."

Wordsters of etymological persuasion also love to track down the origins of phrases. Take the particularly elusive quarry *the whole nine yards.* The fact that no printed citation exists for *the whole nine yards* prior to 1967 renders dubious the nautical theory that the expression refers to the nine sails on a three-square-masted rigger. Nor could *the whole nine yards,* which means "the whole shootin' match," "whole hog," "the whole ball of wax," issue from football, in which a team must gain ten, not nine, yards to reach a first down. Equally unproven or provably wrong are dozens of other etymological explanations, including the material to make a dress, bridal veil, or Scottish kilt; the length of a machine-gun belt in World War II fighter planes; the height of a prison retaining wall; and the volume of mined ore.

My research indicates that *the whole nine yards* refers to the revolving barrels on the backs of concrete mixing trucks. These barrels held a volume of nine cubic yards (they're now twelve cubic yards) in the early 1960s, a fact that explains why I never heard the phrase when I was growing up in the 1950s. Emptying the entire contents was one humungous road job—and, in most states, illegal because the weight of such a load would exceed the per-axel limits.

As you can see, my explanations are never in the abstract—and always in the concrete.

Still another denomination of verbivore sees words as collections of letters to be juggled, shuffled, and flipped. Inspired by the word *bookkeeper,* with its three consecutive pairs of double letters, these logologists fantasize about a biologist who helps maintain raccoon habitats: *a raccoon nook keeper*—six consecutive sets of double letters—and another biologist who studies the liquid secreted by chickadee eggs. They call this scientist a *chickadee egg goo-ologist*—and into the world are born three consecutive pairs of triple letters!

Then there's the breed of logophile who enjoys trying to turn the briar patch of pronoun cases, subject-verb agreement, sequence of tenses, and the indicative and subjunctive moods into a manageable garden of delight. Such devotees of correct usage often explore the nuances of confusing word pairs—*take* vs. *bring* (you take out the garbage; you bring in the newspaper), *podium* vs. *lectern* (you stand on a podium; you stand behind a lectern), and *comprise* vs. *compose* (they're antonyms, not synonyms: the large comprises the small; the large is composed of the small).

Among my favorite wordmongers are those who prowl the lunatic fringes of language—*lunatic* because the ancients believed that prolonged exposure to the moon (Latin *luna*) rendered one moonstruck, or daft. These recreational wordplayers wonder why we drive in a parkway and park in a driveway and why Tiger Woods can drive well on a fairway but not fare well on a driveway. They ponder why our nose can run and our feet can smell, why the third hand on a clock is called the second hand, and why, if adults commit adultery, infants don't commit infantry. Why is it, they muse, that a man puts on a pair of pants but a woman puts on only one bra? Why is it that a man can call a woman a vision, but not a sight—unless his eyes are sore? Then she is a sight for sore eyes.

Finally, there are the legions of pundits, punheads, and pun pals who tell of the Buddhist who said to the hot dog vendor, "Make me one with everything." That's the same Buddhist who never took Novocain when he had teeth drilled, because he wished to transcend dental medication. These punderful verbivores become even bigger hot dogs when they tell about Charlemagne, who mustered his Franks and set out with great relish to assault and pepper the Saracens, but he couldn't catch up. (Frankly, I never sausage a pun. It's the wurst!)

I am heels over head in love with language. When I say *heels over head*, rather than *head over heels,* I am not two letters short of a complete alphabet or a syllable short of a coherent statement. *Head over heels* is the normal position, sort of like doing things ass backwards, which is the way we do everything. I don't know about you, but when I flip over something, my heels are over my head.

When I say *language,* I mean by and large that glorious, uproarious, notorious, outrageous, courageous, contagious, stupendous, tremendous, end-over-endous adventure we call the English language. That's because in matters verbal I am unabashedly lexist. Just as many would say that, among many other things, the Italians do food well and that, among their many other accomplishments, the French do style and fashion well, I believe that we English speakers and writers do language especially well. One might say that we do it lexicellently. This book chronicles my heels-over-head love affair with English. May you have a wordaholic, logoleptic, and verbivorous time sharing that joyride with me.

Richard Lederer
San Diego, California
richard.lederer@pobox.com
www.verbivore.com

A CELEBRATION
OF ENGLISH

Our Abounding English Language

The other day I went to the bookstore to buy a dictionary. The clerk showed me a really cheap one. I couldn't find the words to thank her.

Then she directed me to a thesaurus. I thought that was an accommodating, altruistic, benevolent, caring, compassionate, considerate, courteous, decent, empathic, gracious, kind, magnanimous, nice, obliging, outreaching, solicitous, sweet, sympathetic, and thoughtful thing to do.

The multitudinous choice of words in English offers both a delightful and daunting challenge to native and nonnative speakers. In William Styron's *Sophie's Choice,* the heroine, Polish-born Sophie, expresses mock horror at the infinite variety of English words:

> "Such a language! . . . Too many words. I mean just the word for *velocite.* I mean *fast. Rapid. Quick.* All the same thing! A scandal!"
>
> "*Swift?*" I added.
>
> "How about *speedy?*" Nathan asked.
>
> "*Hasty?*" I went on.
>
> "And *fleet?*" Nathan said. "Though that's a bit fancy."
>
> "Stop it!" Sophie said, laughing." Too much! Too many words, this English. In French it is so simple. You just say *vite.*"

You should not be aghast, amazed, appalled, astonished, astounded, bewildered, blown away, boggled, bowled over, bumfuzzled, caught off base, confounded, dumbfounded, electrified, flabbergasted, floored, flummoxed, overwhelmed, shocked, startled, stunned, stupefied, surprised, taken aback, thrown, or thunderstruck by this o'erflowing cornucopia of synonyms in our marvelous language.

English boasts by far the largest number of words of all languages, 616,500 officially enshrined in the *Oxford English Dictionary*. That's almost four times the vocabulary size of its nearest competitor, German; five times the size of Russian, in third place; and six times the size of Spanish and French, tied for fourth. As a result, English possesses a plethora of synonyms that allow greater nuances of meaning than are available in other tongues.

A much-lauded-and-applauded *New Yorker* cartoon puckishly celebrated our linguistic treasure trove. The cartoon's caption read: "Roget's Brontosaurus," and pictured was a big dinosaur in whose thought bubble appeared: "Large, great, huge, considerable, bulky, voluminous, ample, massive, capacious, spacious, mighty, towering, monstrous . . . ." If not for the finite capacity of thought bubbles, the artist could have added: "big, Brobdingnagian, colossal, enormous, gargantuan, gigantic, grand, hefty, hulking, humongous, husky, immense, jumbo, leviathan, looming, lumbering, mammoth, mountainous, ponderous, prodigious, sizable, substantial, tremendous, vast, weighty, whopping."

Such a cartoon would be far less likely to appear in a magazine printed in a language other than English. Books like *Roget's Thesaurus* are foreign to speakers of most other languages. Given the scope of their vocabularies, they have little need of them.

I hesitate to conclude this song of praise to the glories of English with dark news. But I regret to inform you that yesterday, a senior editor of *Roget's Thesaurus* assumed room temperature, bit the dust, bought the farm, breathed his last, came to the end of the road, cashed in his chips, cooled off, croaked, deep sixed, expired, gave up the ghost, headed for the hearse, headed for the last roundup, kicked off, kicked the bucket, lay down one last time, lay with the lilies, left this mortal plain, met his maker, met Mr. Jordan, passed away, passed in his checks, passed on, perished, permanently changed his address, pulled the plug, pushed up daisies, returned to dust, slipped his cable, slipped his mortal coil, sprouted wings, took the dirt nap, took the long count, pegged out, traveled to kingdom come, turned up his toes, went across the creek, went belly up, went to glory, went the way of all flesh, went to his final reward, went west—and, of course, he died.

Doing a Number
on English

For those who think that our civilization is obsessed with time, the *Concise Oxford English Dictionary* recently added support to that theory by announcing that the word *time* is the most often-used noun in the English language. The dictionary relied on the Oxford English Corpus—a research project into English in the twenty-first century—to come up with the lists.

The Oxford English Corpus gives us the fullest, most accurate picture of the language today. It represents all types of English, from literary novels and specialist journals to everyday newspapers and magazines to the language of chatrooms, e-mails, and Weblogs. And, as English is a global language, used by an estimated one third of the world's population, the Oxford Corpus contains language from all parts of the world—not only from the United Kingdom and the United States, but also from Australia, the Caribbean, Canada, India, Singapore, and South Africa. It is the largest English corpus of its type—the most representative slice of the English language available.

According to the Corpus, *the* is the most commonly used word overall, followed by *be, to, of, and, a, in, that, have,* and *I.* Typical of such frequency lists, the most used words are hardworking function words that hold sentences together. The study also reveals that these ten words and their variations account for 25 percent of all written content.

These top ten are all single-syllable words. In fact, the sixty most frequently used words on the list are monosyllabic, as are ninety-four of the first one hundred. That's because Anglo Saxon concision and simplicity are the heart and soul of our language.

English is the most democratically hospitable language that has ever existed, welcoming words from countries ancient and modern, near and far away. But despite all our loan words, the core of our language remains Anglo-Saxon. Only about 25 percent of our total vocabulary is Anglo-Saxon in origin, but, in most frequency lists, Anglo-Saxon is the source of more than 90 percent of the first hundred words.

Word lists like the Oxford Corpus tell us a great deal about who we English speakers and writers are. While *he* is the sixteenth-most-used word on the list, *she* is thirtieth. While the pronoun *I* comes in at tenth in the Oxford English Corpus, it is first on almost all frequency lists of spoken language.

Focusing on the most frequently occurring nouns in the Oxford Corpus shines a bright light on our values. Among nouns, *person* is ranked second, *man* seventh, *child* twelfth, and *woman* fourteenth. *Government* occupies the twentieth spot on the Oxford Corpus noun list, while *war,* at number forty-nine, trumps *peace*, which did not make the top hundred.

William Shakespeare spoke of people who "run before the clock," as if the hands of the clock would sweep them away if they did not hustle their bustles. In the English-speaking world, so many of us seem to be working harder and taking fewer and shorter vacations. The Oxford English Corpus confirms that obsession with time and productivity by revealing that *time* is the most frequently used noun in our language. *Year* is ranked third, *day* fifth, *work* sixteenth, and *week* seventeenth.

In his poem "To His Coy Mistress," the English poet Andrew Marvell wrote, "But at my back I always hear/Time's winged chariot hurrying near." According to the Oxford English Corpus frequency list, time's winged chariot is running us over.

It is said again and again these days that there are lies, damnable lies, and statistics. Nonetheless, Americans are fascinated with and by statistics and take a special interest in facts that can be quantified. Here are some more insights into our English tongue, expressed statistically:

- Number of languages in the world: Approximately *6,800*, 50 to 90 percent of which will be extinct in a hundred years.
- Number of people around the world who can be reached by English in some form: *1.5 billion.*
- Percentage of those people worldwide who learned English as a second (or third or fourth) language: *52.5.* In other words, first-language English speakers are in the minority. Both China and India have more English speakers than the United States.
- Number of countries or territories in which English has official status: *87.*
- Percentage of the world's English speakers who live in the largest English-speaking country, the United States: *20.*
- Percentage of world English that is American English: *66.*
- Percentage of world English that is British English: *16.*
- Percentage of students in the European Union studying English: *83.*
- Percentage of people in the European Union who are fluent in English: *75.*
- Percentage of nonnative speakers around the world who are fluent in English: *25.*
- Percentage of cyberspace homepages in English: *82*
- Percentage of all books in the world printed in English: *50.*
- Percentage of international telephone calls made in English: *52.*
- Percentage of radio programs worldwide broadcast in English: *60.*
- Percentage of global box office from films in English: *63.*
- Percentage of global e-mail in English: *68.*
- Percentage of international mail and telexes written and addressed in English: *70.*
- Percentage of global computer text stored in English: *80.*
- Percentage of the 12,500 international organizations in the world that make use of the English language: *85.*
- Percentage of those international organizations that use English exclusively: *33.*
- Percentage of all English words throughout history that no longer exist: *85.*
- Number of words listed in the *Oxford English Dictionary,* not counting its supplements: *616,500.*

- Average number of words added to English each year: *1,000*.
- Number of words in the largest dictionaries of German, the world's second largest language: *185,000*.
- Number of words in the largest dictionaries of Russian, the world's third largest language: *130,000*.
- Number of words in the largest dictionaries for French and Spanish, tied for the world's fourth largest language: *100,000*.
- Borrowed words in English versus native (Anglo Saxon) words, expressed as a ratio: *3:1*.
- Number of languages in the English vocabulary: *300*.
- Percentage of English words made from Latin word parts: *50*.
- Number of words the average English speaker actually recognizes: *10,000–20,000*.
- Percentage of the average English speaker's conversation made up of the most frequently used 737 words: *96*.

A Guide to Britspeak, A to Zed

The summer after we were married, my bride, Simone, and I spent ten smashingly lovely honeymoon days on vacation (what the Brits call "holiday") exploring the southwest of Britain. We took a drive and walk through time from the ancient stone mysteries at Stonehenge and Avebury to the modern glitz of Manchester's Granada Studios—Great Britain's answer to our Universal Studios theme park.

Confident that the island natives spoke our language, we expected few communication problems. We did, however, encounter a number of strange words and locutions that you should know when you visit the U.K. (United Kingdom). To clear the fog and unravel some transatlantic tangles, I offer here a selective list of differences between our English and British English. After all, I don't want you to miss the delights of Great Britain just because of a little thing like a language barrier.

If you choose to rent an automobile in the U.K., with it will come a whole new vocabulary. Be sure to fill it with *petrol*, not gas. Remember that the trunk is the boot, the hood is the bonnet (what the Brits call a hood is our convertible top), tires are tyres (and they have tracks, not treads), a headlight is a headlamp, the transmission is the gearbox, the windshield is the windscreen, a fender is a wing, and the muffler is a silencer.

Station wagons (*waggons* in Britspell) that speed by you are called estate cars or hatchbacks, trucks are lorries, and streetcars trams. Most British drivers (motorists) belong to AA—the Automobile Association, of course!

Our buses are their coaches. When a hotel in the British Isles posts a sign proclaiming, "No football coaches allowed," the message is not directed at the Vince Lombardis and Joe Paternos of the world. "No football coaches allowed" means "No soccer buses permitted."

While you are driving down the motorway (highway) and busily converting kilometers into miles, you must note that, in matters automotive, the Queen's English can be as far apart as the lanes on a dual carriageway (divided highway). A traffic circle is a roundabout; an intersection a junction; an overpass a flyover; a circular road around a city is a ringway or orbital; a place to pull off the road, a layby; a road shoulder, a verge; and a railroad (railway) crossing, a level crossing. All the time, you must be sure to stay to the left, not the right! As the joke goes, why did the Siamese twins go to England? Answer: So that the other one could drive.

When you have to use the subway in London, you should follow signs to the underground (informally, the "tube"). When you get on and off the underground, you'll hear a polite voice on the loudspeaker warning you to "mind the gap." That message means "Look out for the space between the train and the platform." As you make your way upward to the streets of London, be aware that "Way out" is not a vestigial hippie expression. "Way out" signifies an exit.

If you decide to walk somewhere, you'll have to bear in mind that what a North American calls a sidewalk is an English pavement, while an American pavement is an English roadway. If someone directs you to the Circus, don't head for a big top. Rather, look for a large circle (Piccadilly Circus is rather like Columbus Circle in New York) where several streets converge.

At the end of World War II, Winston Churchill tells us, the Allied leaders nearly came to blows over a single word during their negotiations when some diplomats suggested that it was time to "table" an important motion. For the British, *table* meant that the motion should be put on the table for discussion. For the Americans it meant just the opposite—that it should be put on the shelf and dismissed from discussion.

Also at the end of the war, the British government made an urgent request for thousands of bushels of corn. So the U.S. government shipped just what the Brits asked for—corn. What the British officials really wanted was wheat. Had they wanted corn, they would have called it "maize" or specified "Indian corn."

Many of the most beguiling misunderstandings can arise where identical words have different meanings in the two cultures and lingoes. When an American exclaims, "I'm mad about my flat," she is upset about her punctured tire. When a Brit exclaims, "I'm mad about my flat," she is exulting about her apartment. When a Brit rails against "that bloody villain," he is describing the dastard's immoral character, not his physical condition. When a Brit points out that you have "a ladder in your hose," the situation is not as bizarre as you might at first think. Quite simply, you have a run in your stocking.

Some of this bilingual confusion can get downright embarrassing: When Brits tell you that they will "come by in the morning and knock you up," they are informing you that they will wake you up with a knock on your door. (Similarly, *a knock up* in tennis means, simply, to hit the ball around.)

When a Brit offers to show you his collection of bloomers, he means his examples of bloopers, or verbal faux pas. When a Londoner wants to take you "to the BM," she is talking about the British Museum. When a Brit volunteers to take you to a solicitor, that's a trip to a general-practice lawyer. When a Brit asks you if you need a rubber, she is trying to make your writing safer. English rubbers are erasers. When a Brit tells you how marvelously "homely" you are, that's a compliment. He means that you are domestic and home-loving. In the UK it is quite possible to be both homely and attractive at the same time.

In the early part of this century, Finley Peter Dunne's Mr. Dooley wryly observed, "When the American people get through with the English language, it will look as if it has been run over by a musical comedy." And as recently as 1974, Morton Cooper sneered meanly that "giving the English language to the Americans is like giving sex to small children; they know it's important, but they don't know what to do with it." A message on a London theater (theatre) marquee went so far as to advertise, "American Western Film - English subtitles." A London store sign announced, "English spoken here—American understood."

With the increasing influence of film, radio, television, and international travel, the two main streams of the English language are rapidly converging like the streets of a circus. Still, there are scores of words, phrases, spellings, and constructions about which Brits and

Yanks just don't agree. During a transatlantic telephone conversation, one of my British publishers told me that my book was attracting considerable newspaper coverage and she would be sure to send me the "cuttings." I asked her what she called the sections of plants one gets from gardens. She answered, "Those are clippings, of course." Of course—and not surprising in a land where the beer and Coke are warm and the toast is cold.

Here's a pop quiz that will help you discover how "bilingual" you are. Answers repose on page 140.

1. Look over these words and compound words that occur in both Britspeak and American. Then ask yourself what each one means in British English: *billion, biscuit, bitter, bob, braces, catapult, chemist, chips, crisp, dinner jacket, full stop, ground floor, hockey, ice, jelly, knickers, lift, M.P., minister, plaster, pocketbook, public school, pudding, spectacles, stone, stuff, sweet, till, tin, torch, vest, waistcoat.*

2. What would the average Brit call each of these words and compounds?: *aisle, bar, bathroom, bobby pin, clothespin, counterclockwise, hardware store, intermission, kerosene, napkin, quilt, shrimp, silverware, sled, swimsuit, telephone booth, thumbtack,* the letter *z.*

3. What is the American equivalent of each of the following Briticisms?: *advert, banger, bobby, chucker-out, don, draughts, dressing gown, dustbin, fortnight, hoover, plimsolls, porridge, pram, scone, spanner, starter, switchback, takeaway, telly.*

4. The *Dictionary of British Pronunciation with American Variants* shows differences in the pronunciation of 28 percent of the words therein. The broad *a* of *ahsk* and *clahss* is probably the most familiar mark of "educated" British speech, even though the flat *a* that most Americans use is actually the older of the two pronunciations. How would a speaker with the so-called standard (or received) British accent pronounce these words?: *ate, been, bone, clerk, duty, either, evolution, fear, figure, garage, herb, laboratory, leisure, lieutenant, missile, patriot, privacy, schedule, secretary, suggest, tomato (and potato), vitamin, zebra.*

5. The writing of the two languages shows such differences in spelling that it is practically impossible to go through a single page without being made aware of the writer's nationality. The most obvious divergence is in words that end in *-or* in American but

-our in Britain—*behaviour, flavour, harbour, honour, labour, odour,* and *vigour*. Perhaps you have noticed the credit that pops up in many British films: "Colour by Technicolor."

How would these words be spelled in British English?: *airplane, aluminum, check, defense, fiber, gray, inflection, inquire, jail, jewelry, judgment, maneuver, marvelous, organization, pajamas, plow, program, specialty, spelled, story* (floor of a building), *tons, vial, whiskey.*

6. Some differences exist between British and American usage. In what form is each of the following constructions and idioms likely to appear in British English? *China is leading the world in exports; different from; in the hospital; living on Baker Street.*

THIS AMERICAN LANGUAGE

A Declaration
of Language
Independence

Beginning with the Pilgrims, the story of language in America is the story of our Declaration of Linguistic Independence, the separating from its parent of that magnificent upstart we call American English.

John Adams was one of the first to lead the charge for American linguistic autonomy. In 1780, sixteen years before he became president, he called upon Congress to establish an academy for "correcting, improving, and ascertaining the English language." "English," Adams proclaimed, "is destined to be in the next and succeeding centuries more generally the language of the world than Latin was in the last or French is in the present age. The reason of this is obvious, because the increasing population in America, and their universal connection and correspondence with all nations, will, aided by the influence of England in the world, whether great or small, force their language into general use."

At the time Adams made that prediction, an obscure Connecticut schoolmaster was soon to become a one-man academy of American English. His name, now synonymous with the word *dictionary,* was Webster. Noah Webster (1758–1843) saw the untapped promise of the new republic. He was afire with the conviction that a United States no longer politically dependent on England should also become independent in language. In his *Dissertations on the English Language,* published in 1789, Webster declared linguistic war on the King's

English: "As an independent nation, our honor requires us to have a system of our own, in language as well as government. Great Britain, whose children we are, and whose language we speak, should no longer be our standard; for the taste of her writers is already corrupted, and her language on the decline."

In putting his vision into practice, Noah Webster traveled throughout America, listening to people's speech and taking detailed notes. He included in his dictionaries an array of shiny new American words, among them *applesauce, bullfrog, chowder, handy, hickory, succotash, tomahawk*—and *skunk:* "a quadruped remarkable for its smell." Webster also proudly used quotations by Americans to illustrate and clarify many of his definitions. The likes of Ben Franklin, George Washington, John Jay, and Washington Irving took their places as authorities alongside William Shakespeare, John Milton, and the Bible. In shaping the American language, Webster also taught a new nation a new way to spell. He deleted the *u* from words such as *honour* and *labour* and the *k* from words such as *musick* and *publick,* he reversed the last two letters in words such as *centre* and *theatre,* and he Americanized the spelling of words such as *plough* and *gaol.*

Perhaps no one has celebrated this "American dialect" with more passion and vigor than the poet Walt Whitman. "The Americans are going to be the most fluent and melodious-voiced people in the world—and the most perfect users of words," he predicted before the Civil War. "The new world, the new times, the new people, the new vistas need a new tongue. What is more, they will . . . not be satisfied until it is evolved."

More than a century later, it's debatable whether Americans are "the most fluent and melodious-voiced people in the world," but there is no question that we are still engaged in the American Evolution and that our American parlance is as rollicking and pyrotechnic as ever. Consider our invention, in the past fifty years, of delectables on the order of *carbon footprint, couch potato, mouse potato* (a couch potato attached to a computer), *digerati, hottie, humongous, ginormous, sleazebag, soccer mom, d'oh, OMG,* and *unfriend.*

From the Age of Queen Anne (1702–1714), the British have thundered against what one of their magazines called "the torrent of barbarous phraseology" that poured from the American colonies.

The first British broadside launched against an Americanism is recorded in 1735, when an English visitor named Francis Moore referred to the young city of Savannah as standing upon a hill overlooking a river "which they in barbarous English call a bluff."

The British were still beating their breasts over what the *Monthly Mirror* called "the corruptions and barbarisms which are hourly obtaining in the speech of our trans-Atlantic colonies," long after we stopped being colonies. They objected to almost every term that they did not consider standard English, protesting President Jefferson's use of the verb *belittle.* They expressed shock at the American tendency to employ, in place of *suppose,* the likes of *expect, reckon, calculate,* and—a special target—*guess,* conveniently overlooking Geoffrey Chaucer's centuries-old "Of twenty yeer of age he was, I gesse."

Returning from a tour through the United States in the late nineteenth century, the playwright Oscar Wilde jested, "We really have everything in common with America nowadays except, of course, language." Wilde's fellow playwright George Bernard Shaw observed, "England and America are two countries separated by a common language."

But our homegrown treasure Mark Twain put it all into perspective when he opined about American English, as compared with British English: "The property has gone into the hands of a joint stock company, and we own the bulk of the shares."

Talking Turkey

As the (probably apocryphal) tale spins out, back in the early colonial days, a white hunter and a friendly Native American made a pact before they started out on the day's hunt. Whatever they bagged was to be divided equally between them. At the end of the day, the white man undertook to distribute the spoils, consisting of several buzzards and turkeys. He suggested to his fellow hunter, "Either I take the turkeys and you the buzzards, or you take the buzzards and I take the turkeys." At this point the Native American complained, "You talk buzzard to me. Now talk turkey." And ever since, *to talk turkey* has meant "to tell it like it is."

Let's talk turkey about our Native American heritage. Suppose you had been one of the early explorers or settlers of North America. You would have found many things in your new land unknown to you. The handiest way of filling voids in your vocabulary would have been to ask local Native Americans what words they used. The early colonists began borrowing words from friendly Indians almost from the moment of their first contact, and many of those names have remained in our everyday language:

Food: *squash* (Narraganset), *pecan* (Algonquian), *hominy* (Algonquian), *pone* (Algonquian), *pemmican* (Cree), and *succotash* (Narraganset);

People: *sachem* (Narraganset), *squaw* (Massachuset), *papoose* (Narraganset), and *mugwump* (Natick);

Daily life: *moccasin* (Chippewa), *toboggan* (Algonquian), *tomahawk* (Algonquian), *wigwam* (Abenaki), *teepee* (Dakota), *caucus* (Algonquian), *powwow* (Narraganset), *wampum* (Massachuset), *bayou* (Choctaw), *potlatch* (Chinook), *hogan* (Navajo), *hickory* (Algonquian), *kayak* (Inuit), *parka* (Aleut), and *totem* (Ojibwa).

Pronouncing many of the Native American words was difficult for the early explorers and settlers. In many instances, they had to shorten and simplify the names. Given the Native American names, identify the following animals: *apossoun, otchock, rahaugcum,* and *segankw.*

The hidden animals are: *opossum* (Algonquian), *woodchuck* (Narraganset), *raccoon* (Algonquian), and *skunk* (Algonquian). To this menagerie we may add the likes of *caribou* (Micmac), *chipmunk* (Ojibwa), *moose* (Algonquian), *muskrat* (Abenaki), and *porgy* (Algonquian).

If you look at a map of the United States, you will realize how freely settlers used words of Indian origin to name the places where we live. Rivers, lakes, ponds, creeks, mountains, valleys, counties, towns, and cities as large as Chicago (from a Fox word that means "place that stinks of onions" or from another Indian word that means "great, powerful") bear Native American names. Four of our five Great Lakes—Huron, Ontario, Michigan, and Erie—and twenty-five of our states have names that were borrowed from Native American words:

Alabama: name of a tribe in the Creek Confederacy; *Alaska:* mainland (Aleut); *Arizona:* place of the little springs (Papago); *Arkansas:* downstream people (Sioux); *Connecticut:* place of the long river (Algonquian);

Idaho: behold the sun coming down the mountains (Shoshone); *Illinois:* superior people (Illini); *Iowa:* beautiful land (Ioway); *Kansas:* south wind people (Sioux); *Kentucky:* meadowland (Cherokee);

Massachusetts: great hill place (Massachuset); *Michigan:* great water (Chippewa); *Minnesota:* milky blue water (Sioux); *Mississippi:* father of waters (Ojibwa); *Missouri:* people of the large canoes (Fox);

Nebraska: flat water (Sioux); *North Dakota* and *South Dakota:* named for the Dakota tribe; *Ohio:* great river (Iroquois); *Oklahoma:* red people (Choctaw);

Tennessee: name of a Cherokee village; *Texas:* friends (Tejas); *Utah:* name of a Ute tribe; *Wisconsin:* gathering of waters (Algonquian); *Wyoming:* large prairie place (Delaware);

Some of our loveliest place names began life as Native American words—Susquehanna, Shenandoah, Rappahannock. Such names are the stuff of poetry. To the poet Walt Whitman, Monongahela "rolls with venison richness upon the palate." William Penn wrote about the Leni-Lenape Indians: "I know not a language spoken in Europe that hath words of more sweetness and greatness." How fortunate we are that the poetry the First Peoples heard in the American landscape lives on in our American language.

All-American Dialects

From California to the New York island, from the redwood forest to the Gulf Stream waters, I hear America singing. We are teeming nations within a nation, a nation that is like a world. We talk in melodies of infinite variety; we dance to their sundry measures and lyrics.

Midway through John Steinbeck's epic novel *The Grapes of Wrath,* young Ivy observes, "Ever'body says words different. Arkansas folks says 'em different, and Oklahomy folks says 'em different. And we seen a lady from Massachusetts, an' she said 'em differentest of all. Couldn't hardly make out what she was sayin.'"

One aspect of American rugged individualism is that not all of us say the same word in the same way. Sometimes we don't even use the same name for the same object. I was born and grew up in Philadelphia a coon's age, a blue moon, and a month of Sundays ago, when Hector was a pup. *Phillufia,* or *Philly,* which is what we kids called the city, was where the Epicurean delight made with cold cuts, cheese, tomatoes, lettuce, pickles, and onions stuffed into a long, hard-crusted Italian bread loaf was invented.

The creation of that sandwich took place in the Italian pushcart section of the city, known as Hog Island. Some linguists contend that it was but a short leap from *Hog Island* to *hoagie,* while others claim that the label *hoagie* arose because only a hog had the appetite or the technique to eat one properly.

As a young adult I moved to northern New England (*N'Hampsha,* to be specific), where the same sandwich designed to be a meal in itself is called a grinder, because you need a good set of grinders to chew it. But my travels around the United States have revealed that the hoagie or grinder is called at least a dozen other names—a bomber, Garibaldi (after the Italian liberator), hero, Italian sandwich, rocket, sub, submarine (which is what they call it in California), torpedo, wedge, wedgie, and, in the deep South, a poor-boy (usually pronounced "poh-boy").

In Philadelphia, we wash our hoagies down with soda. In New England we do it with tonic, and by that word I don't mean medicine. Soda and tonic in other parts are known as pop, soda pop, soft drink, Coke, and quinine.

In northern New England, they take the term *milk shake* quite literally. To many residing in that little corner of the country, a milk shake consists of milk mixed with flavored syrup—and nothing more—shaken up until foamy. If you live in Rhode Island or in southern Massachusetts and you want ice cream in your milk drink, you ask for a cabinet (named after the square wooden cabinet in which the mixer was encased). If you live farther north, you order a velvet or a frappe (from the French *frapper,* "to ice").

Clear—or is it clean? or is it plumb?—across the nation, Americans sure do talk "different."

What do you call those flat, doughy things you often eat for breakfast—battercakes, flannel cakes, flapjacks, griddle cakes, or pancakes?

Is that simple strip of grass between the street and the sidewalk a berm, boulevard, boulevard strip, city strip, devil strip, green belt, the parking, parking strip, parkway, sidewalk plot, strip, swale, tree bank, or tree lawn?

Is the part of the highway that separates the northbound lanes from the southbound lanes the center strip, mall, medial strip, median strip, medium strip, or neutral ground?

Is it a cock horse, dandle, hicky horse, horse, horse tilt, ridy horse, seesaw, teeter, teeterboard, teetering board, teetering horse, teetertotter, tilt, tilting board, tinter, tinter board, or tippity bounce?

Do fisherpersons employ an angledog, angleworm, baitworm, earthworm, eaceworm, fishworm, mudworm, rainworm, or redworm? Is a larger worm a dew worm, night crawler, night walker, or town worm?

Is it a crabfish, clawfish, craw, crawdab, crawdad, crawdaddy, crawfish, crawler, crayfish, creekcrab, crowfish, freshwater lobster, ghost shrimp, mudbug, spiny lobster, or yabby?

Depends where you live and whom it is you're talking to.

I figger, figure, guess, imagine, opine, reckon, and suspect that my being bullheaded, contrary, headstrong, muley, mulish, ornery, otsny, pigheaded, set, sot, stubborn, or utsy about this whole matter of dialects makes you sick to, in, or at your stomach.

But I assure you that, when it comes to American dialects, I'm not speaking flapdoodle, flumaddiddle, flummydiddle, or flurriddiddle. I'm no all-thumbs-and-no-fingers, all-knees-and-elbows, all-left-feet, all-hat-and-no-cattle, antigoddling, bumfuzzled, discombobulated, frustrated, foozled bumpkin, clodhopper, country jake, hayseed, hick, hillbilly, Hoosier, jackpine savage, mossback, mountain-boomer, pumpkin-husker, rail-splitter, rube, sodbuster, stump farmer, swamp angel, yahoo, or yokel.

If you ask most adults what a dialect is, they will tell you it's what somebody else in another region passes off as English. These regions tend to be exotic places like Mississippi or Texas—or Brooklyn, where *oil* is a rank of nobility and *earl* is a black, sticky substance.

If the truth be told, we all have accents. Many New Englanders drop the *r* in *cart* and *farm* and say *caht* and *fahm*. Thus, the Midwesterner's "park the car in Harvard Yard" becomes the New Englander's "pahk the cah in Hahvahd Yahd." But those *r*'s aren't lost. A number of upper-class Northeasterners add *r*'s to words, such as *idear* and *Chiner* when those words come before a vowel or at the end of a sentence.

The most widespread of American dialects is that spoken across the South. It's reported that many Southerners reacted to the elections of Jimmy Carter and Bill Clinton by saying, "Well, at last we have a president who talks without an accent."

Actually, Southerners, like everyone else, do speak with an accent, as witness these tongue-in-cheek entries in *A Dictionary of Southernisms*:

ah: organ for seeing
are: sixty minutes
arn: ferrous metal
ass: frozen water
ast: questioned
bane: small, kidney-shaped vegetable
bar: seek and receive a loan; a grizzly

bold: heated in water
card: one who lacks courage
farst: a lot of trees
fur: distance
har: to employ
hep: to assist
hire yew: a greeting
paw tree: verse
rat: opposite of *left*
rats: what the Constitution guarantees us
reckanize: to see
retard: stopped working at the job
seed: past tense of *saw*
tar: a rubber wheel
tarred: exhausted
t'mar: day following *t'day*
thang: item
thank: to cogitate
y'all: a bunch of *you*'s

Each language is a great pie. Each slice of that pie is a dialect, and no single slice is the language.

In the early 1960s, John Steinbeck decided to rediscover America in a camper with his French poodle, Charley. The writer reported his observations in *Travels with Charley* and included these thoughts on American dialects:

One of my purposes was to listen, to hear speech, accent, speech rhythms, overtones, and emphasis. For speech is so much more than words and sentences. I did listen everywhere. It seemed to me that regional speech is in the process of disappearing, not gone but going. Forty years of radio and twenty years of television must have this impact. Communications must destroy localness by a slow, inevitable process.

I can remember a time when I could almost pinpoint a man's place of origin by his speech. That is growing more difficult now and will in some foreseeable future become impossible. It is a rare house or building that is not rigged with spiky combers of the air. Radio and television speech becomes standardized, perhaps better English than we have ever used. Just as our bread, mixed and baked, packaged and sold without benefit of accident or human frailty, is uniformly good and uniformly tasteless, so will our speech become one speech.

More than a half century has passed since Steinbeck made that observation, and the hum and buzz of electronic voices have since permeated almost every home across our nation. Formerly, the psalmist tells us, "The voice of the turtle was heard in the land." Now it is the voice of the broadcaster, with his or her immaculately groomed diction. Let us hope that American English does not turn into a bland, homogenized, pasteurized, assembly-line product. May our bodacious American English remain tasty and nourishing—full of flavor, variety, and local ingredients.

Slang As It Is Slung

Slang is hot and slang is cool. Slang is righteous and slang is wicked. Slang is the bee's knees, the cat's meow, the cat's whiskers, and the cat's pajamas. Slang is swell, ducky, peachy keen, super, tops, nifty, far out, groovy, hip, excellent, endsville, flipville, copacetic, outasight, and totally tubular. Slang is fresh, fly, phat, fabulous, fantabulous, uber—da bomb. Slang is ace, awesome, bad, sweet, smooth, sassy, unreal, primo, fab, gear, tuff, the most, the max. Slang is beast, boss, dope, tite, mint, neat, neato, nasty, fetch, chill, cool beans, ice cold, large, rad, sick, sickening, ill, killer, def, epic, chunky, cretaceous, whoa, and like wow! Slang is smokin', blazin', kickin', cruisin', scoopin', stylin', bitchin', bangin', pimpin', slammin', frickin' A, bomb-ass, and kick-ass.

That's more than eighty ways of saying that, if variety is the spice of life, slang is the spice of language. Slang adds gusto to the feast of words, as long as speakers and writers remember that too much spice can kill the feast of any dish.

What is slang? In the preface to their *Dictionary of American Slang*, Harold Wentworth and Stuart Berg Flexner define slang as "the body of words and expressions frequently used by or intelligible to a rather large portion of the general American public, but not accepted as good, formal usage by the majority." Slang, then, is seen as a kind of vagabond language that prowls the outskirts of respectable speech, yet few of us can get along without it. Even our statespersons have a hard time getting by without such colloquial or slang expressions as *hit the nail on the head, team effort, pass the buck*, and *talk turkey*.

Nobody is quite sure where the word *slang* comes from. According to H. L. Mencken, *slang* developed in the eighteenth century (it was first recorded in 1756) either from an erroneous past tense of *sling (sling-slang-slung)* or from the word *language* itself, as in *(thieve)s'lang(uage)* and *(beggar)s'lang(*uage). The second theory makes the point that jargon and slang originate and are used by a particular trade or class group, but slang words come to be slung around to some extent by a whole population.

The use of slang is far more ancient than the word *slang* itself. In fact, slang is nearly as old as language itself, and in all languages at all times some slang expressions have entered the main stream of the vocabulary to pollute or enrich, depending on one's view of the matter. We find traces of slang in the Sanskrit of ancient India, where writers amused themselves now and then by calling a head a "dish." In Latin literary records we discover, alongside *caput*, the standard term for "head," the word *testa*, which meant "pot" or "jug." Both the Sanskrit "dish" and the Latin "pot" share the flavor of our modern *crackpot, jughead*, and *mug*.

The fourteenth-century poet Geoffrey Chaucer used *gab* for "talk" and *bones* for "dice," exactly as we employ them today. William Shakespeare, the literary lord of stage and classroom, coined *costard* (a large apple) to mean "head" and *clay-brained* and *knotty pated* to mean "slow of wit." We discover "laugh yourself into stitches" in *Twelfth Night*, "not so hot" in *The Winter's Tale*, and "right on" in *Julius Caesar*.

There are some very human reasons why the river of slang courses through every language. One of them is that people like novelty and variety in their lives and in their language. To satisfy this urge, they continuously coin new slang words and expressions. This small disquisition began with eighty breezy ways of saying "wonderful," but that feat pales next to the 2,964 synonyms for *drunk* that Paul Dickson trots out in his book *Drunk*—from the euphemistic *tired* to the comical *plastered*, from the nautical *afloat* to the erudite *Bacchi-plenus*, from the elegant *inebriated* to the scatological *shit-faced,* and from the terminal *stiff* to the uncategorizable *zoozled*.

Second, slang allows us to break the ice and shift into a more casual and friendly gear. "What's cooking?" or "How's it going?" sound more easygoing and familiar than "How do you do?" "Slang," said Carl Sandburg, is "language that rolls up its sleeves, spits on its hands, and gets to work."

A third motive is sheer playfulness. Slang such as *rubbernecker* for a sightseer in a car and *motormouth* for someone who gabs on and on, and reduplications such as *heebie-jeebies* and *okey dokey* tickle our sense of humor.

Finally, as G. K. Chesterton proclaimed, "All slang is metaphor, and all metaphor is poetry." American slang abounds in fresh figures of speech that evoke arresting word pictures in the mind's eye. We intellectually understand "an angry, persecuted husband," but the slanguage version "a henpecked husband stewing in his own juice" takes a vivid shortcut to our imagination.

An English professor announced to the class, "There are two words I don't allow in my class. One is *gross* and the other is *cool*." From the back of the room a voice called out, "So, what are the two words?" Slang is a powerful stimulant that keeps our American language alive and growing. Slang is a prominent part of our American wordscape. In fact, the *Dictionary of American Slang* estimates that slang makes up perhaps a fifth of the words we use. Many of our most valuable and pungent words have begun their lives keeping company with thieves, vagrants, and hipsters.

The Circus of Words

"**H**ey, First-of-May! Tell the butcher in the backyard to stay away from the bulls, humps, stripes, and painted ponies. We have some cherry pie for him before doors and spec." Sound like doubletalk? Actually, it's circus talk—or, more technically, circus argot, argot being a specialized vocabulary used by a particular group for mutual bonding and private communication. Communities are most likely to develop a colorful argot when they have limited contact with the world outside of their group. The circus community is a perfect example of the almost monastic self-containment in which argot flourishes. Big-top people travel in very close quarters, and because they usually go into a town, set up, do a show, tear down, and leave, they have little contact with the locals. They socialize with each other, they intermarry, and their children acquire the argot from the time they start to talk.

First-of-May designates anyone who is brand-new to circus work. That's because circuses used to start their tours around the first day in May. A *candy butcher* is a concessionaire who sells cotton candy (*floss*) and other food, along with drinks and souvenirs, to the audience during the show. The *backyard* is the place just behind the circus entrance where performers wait to do their acts. A *bull* is a circus elephant, even though most of them are female. Among other circus beasts, *humps, stripes,* and *painted ponies* are, respectively, camels, tigers, and zebras. *Cherry pie* is extra work, probably from *chairy pie,* the setting up of extra chairs around the arena. *Doors!* is the cry that tells circus folk that the audience is coming in to take their seats, and *spec* is short for *spectacle,* the big parade of all the performers.

Trust me: This topic ain't no *dog and pony show*—the designation for a small circus with just a few acts, also known as a *mud show.*

What we call the toilet circus folk call the *donniker,* the hot dog or grill concession trailer where the circus can snag a snack is a *grease joint,* and a circus performer is a *kinker.* The townspeople are *towners* or *rubes.* In the old days, when large groups of towners who believed (sometimes accurately) that they had been fleeced by dishonest circus people, they would come back in a mob to seek retribution. The cry *Hey rube!* went out, and everyone knew that the fight was on.

A full house is called a *straw house* from the days when straw would be laid down in front of the seats to accommodate more people than the seats could hold. Distances between engagements were called *jumps.* Thus, an old circus toast rings out: "May your lots be grassy, your jumps short, and your houses straw."

Words from
Our Presidents

What may be the most useful expression of universal communication ever devised, *OK* is recognizable and pronounceable in almost every language on earth.

The explanations for the origin of *OK* have been as imaginative as they have been various. But the late Columbia University professor and language maven Allen Walker Read proved that *OK* did not derive from *okeh,* an affirmative reply in Choctaw; nor from the name of chief Old Keokuk; nor from a fellow named Orrin Kendall, who manufactured a tasty brand of army biscuit for Union soldiers in the Civil War and stamped them *OK*; nor from the Haitian port Aux Cayes, which produced superior rum; nor from "open key," a telegraph term; nor from the Greek *ola kalla,* meaning "all good."

Rather, as Professor Read pointed out, the truth is more political than any of these theories. He tracked down the first known published appearance of *OK* with its current meaning in the Boston *Morning Post* on March 23, 1839: "The 'Chairman of the Committee on Charity Lecture Balls' is one of the deputation, and perhaps if he should return to Boston, via Providence, he of the Journal, and his train-band, would have the 'contribution box,' et ceteras, o.k.—all correct—and cause the corks to fly, like sparks, upward."

Doctor Read demonstrated that *OK* started life as an obscure joke and through a twist of fate went to the top of the charts on the American hit parade of words. In the 1830s, in New England, there was a craze for initialisms, in the manner of *LOL, OMG, aka,* and *TGIF,* so popular today. The fad went so far as to generate letter combinations of intentionally comic misspellings: *KG* for "know go,"

KY for "know yuse," *NSMJ* for "'nough said 'mong jentlemen," and *OR* for "oll rong." *OK* for "oll korrect" naturally followed.

Of all those loopy initialisms and jocular misspellings *OK* alone survived. That's because of a presidential nickname that consolidated the letters in the national memory. Martin Van Buren, elected our eighth president in 1836, was born in Kinderhook, New York, and, early in his political career, was dubbed "Old Kinderhook." Echoing the "oll korrect" initialism, *OK* became the rallying cry of the Old Kinderhook Club, a Democratic organization supporting Van Buren during the 1840 campaign. Thus, the accident of Van Buren's birthplace rescued *OK* from the dustbin of history.

The coinage did Van Buren no good, and he was defeated in his bid for reelection. But *OK* has become what H. L. Mencken identified as "the most shining and successful Americanism ever invented."

* * *

Mothers sewed stuffed bears before President Theodore Roosevelt came along, but no one called them teddy bears. Not until November, 1902, when the president went on a bear hunt in Smedes, Mississippi.

Roosevelt was acting as adjudicator for a border dispute between the states of Louisiana and Mississippi. On November 14, during a break in the negotiations, he was invited by southern friends to go bear hunting. Roosevelt felt that he could consolidate his support in the South by appearing there in the relaxed atmosphere of a hunting party, so he accepted the invitation.

During the hunt, Roosevelt's hosts cornered a bear cub, and a guide roped it to a tree for the president to kill. Roosevelt declined to shoot the cub, believing such an act to be beneath his dignity as a hunter and as a man: "If I shot that little fellow I couldn't be able to look my boys in the face again."

That Sunday's *Washington Post* carried a cartoon, drawn by Clifford Berryman (1869–1949), of President Theodore Roosevelt. T.R. stood in hunting gear, rifle in hand, and his back turned toward the cowering cub. The caption read, "Drawing the line in Mississippi," referring both to the border dispute and to animal ethics.

Now the story switches to the wilds of Brooklyn, New York. There Russian immigrants Morris and Rose Michtom owned a candy store where they sold handmade stuffed animals. Inspired by Berryman's cartoon, Rose Michtom made a toy bear and displayed it in the shop window. The bear proved wildly popular with the public.

The Michtoms sent President Roosevelt the very bear they had put in their window. They said it was meant for Roosevelt's grandchildren and asked T.R. for permission to confer linguistic immortality upon him. The president replied, "I don't know what my name may mean to the bear business but you're welcome to use it."

Rose and Morris began turning out stuffed cubs labeled *Teddy's bear*, in honor of our twenty-sixth president. As the demand increased, the family hired extra seamstresses and rented a warehouse. Their operation eventually became the Ideal Toy Corporation.

The bear was a prominent emblem in Roosevelt's successful 1904 election campaign, and *Teddy's bear* was enshrined in dictionaries in 1907. Cartoonist Berryman never sought compensation for the many uses of the cub he had created. He simply smiled and said, "I have made thousands of children happy; that is enough for me."

Stamp Out Fadspeak!

Some people lament that speaking and writing these days are simply a collection of faddish clichés patched together like the sections of prefabricated houses made of ticky-tacky. They see modern communication as a mindless clacking of trendy expressions, many of them from movies and television sitcoms.

Why is English parlance in such a parlous state? Maybe it's because verbal knee-jerkery requires no thought. It's so much easier not to think, isn't it? It's so much easier to cookie-cut the rich dough of the English language. It's so much easier to microwave a frozen dinner than to create a meal from scratch. After all, when we were children, we loved to pull the string on the doll that said the same thing over and over, again and again.

That's what fadspeak is—the unrelenting mix of mimicry and gimmickry. Fadspeak comprises vogue phrases that suddenly appear on everybody's tongues—phrases that launch a thousand lips. Before you can say, "yada yada yada," these throwaway expressions become instant clichés, perfect for our throwaway society, like paper wedding dresses for throwaway marriages. Fadspeak clichés lead mayfly lives, counting their duration in months instead of decades. They strut and fret their hour upon the stage of pop culture and then are heard no more.

To demonstrate, I offer here a narrative composed almost entirely of clichés, not just any clichés but fadspeak clichés that have slithered into our language just in the last decade or two or three. That I can actually cobble together a coherent rant composed of new clichés is, I believe, a sad tribute to the ascendancy of fadspeak. OMG, how cool is that?

Hey, would I, your deep-pockets, drop-dead-good-looking language columnist, your poster boy for user-friendly writing, ever serve you anything totally bogus like fadspeak? I don't think so. Not a problem. I have zero tolerance for anything that lowers the bar for what makes world-class writing.

Work with me on this. I've been around the block, and I know a thing or two. I know that I wear many hats, but I'm not talking trash here. I'm not the eight-hundred-pound gorilla out to bust your chops. I feel your pain, and I'm your new best friend. At this point in time, you're on my radar, and I know you da man! Yessss!

Hey, people, this isn't rocket science or brain surgery. Call me crazy, but it's simply a no-brainer—a dropkick and a slam dunk. I, the mother of all language mavens, will go to the mat 24-7 for fresh, original language. You know what? I'm my own toughest critic, so I get more bang for the buck when I avoid those new clichés. I want to do the heavy lifting, level the playing field, and give something back to the community. Join the club. Do the math. Get used to it. It works for me. Welcome to my world.

So I'm making you an offer you can't refuse. Maybe it's TMI, but I'm never going to slip into those hackneyed, faddish expressions that afflict our precious American language. Having said that, how about we run that one up the flagpole and see who salutes? Sound like a plan? It's a done deal because I've got a full plate and I bring a lot to the table. I come to play, and the ball's in your court.

Sheesh. Get over it. Doesn't it push your buttons, yank your chain, and rattle your cage when a writer or speaker puts dynamite language on the back burner? Doesn't it send you on an emotional roller coaster until you crash and burn when they try to put a good face on it? Doesn't fadspeak just blow you out of the water and make you want to scream, "Oh, puh-leeze! In your dreams! Excuuuuse me! It's my way or the highway! Why are you shooting yourself in the foot? You're history! You're toast! You're going down! That's so twentieth century! Put a sock in it! Don't give up your day job!"?

As for me, I'm like, "Are you the writer from hell? You are all over the map. You are like a deer caught in the headlights. Lose the attitude, man. You are so-o-o-o busted. Read my lips! Maybe it's a guy thing, but get real! Get an attitude adjustment. Get with the twenty-first century! Get a life! And while you're at it, why don't you knock yourself out and get a vocabulary?" Be afraid. Be very afraid.

Anyhoo, off the top of my head, the bottom line is that fadspeakers and fadwriters—and you know who you are—are so clueless.

I am shocked—shocked!—that they just don't suck it up, get up to speed, go the whole nine yards, push the envelope, take it to another level, and think outside the box. All they do is give you that same-old-same-old, been-there-done-that kind of writing, and you can take that to the bank.

Tell me about it. Fadspeakers and fadwriters just play the old tapes again and again, and their ideas just fall through the cracks. They're sooo clueless. They're not playing with a full deck. The light's on, but nobody's home. Elvis has left the building. Ya think? Go figure.

Hel-loh? Earth to clichémeisters. Duuuh. Boooring. What's wrong with this picture? Are we on the same page? Are we having fun yet? Are you having some kind of a bad-hair day? Are you having a midlife crisis? A senior moment? Maybe it's time for a wake-up call? Or maybe a reality check? I don't think so. In your dreams. Not even close.

O-o-k-a-a-y. You wanna talk about it? You wanna get with the program? Why don't you man up, wake up, and smell the coffee? How about we cut right to the chase? I mean, what part of "fad-speak" don't you understand? Deal with it. You got that right. Or maybe I'm just preaching to the choir.

Whatever. As if. At the end of the day, it is what it is.

Now that I've got your attention, here's the buzz on viable, cut-ting-edge communication. Whenever I find some of these snippets of fadspeak strewn about a sentence, I'm in your face. I'm your worst nightmare. Those flavor-of-the-month phrases just make me go bal-listic, even to the point of going postal. After all—and I'm not making this up—what goes around comes around.

All right. My bad. I understand that you're not a happy camper, and maybe you just don't want to go there. But I do because I've got all my ducks in a row. I mean, is this a great language—or what? I mean, it's a language to die for. I mean, if they can put a man on the moon, why can't they teach people to write well?

Gimme a break. Cut me some slack. What am I, chopped liver? Hey, what do I know? I'm just old school. And now that I've thrown my hissy fit about fadspeak, here's what's going down.

We're done now. Thanks a bunch for letting me share. Now that I've been able to tell it like it is, it's time to pack it in. I'm outa here. Talk to you soon. Buh-bye—and have a nice day.

Like, What's Happening to Our Language?

In one of the megachain bookstores, a woman asked a young clerk for the author of *Like Water for Chocolate*. After the salesperson had spent five minutes searching and still could not locate the famous title, the customer realized that the young man had been looking for *Water from Chocolate*.

It's like . . . you know.

Nowadays two speech patterns of the younger generation squeak like chalk across the blackboard of adult sensibilities—the sprinkling of *like* throughout sentences, like, you know what I'm saying, and the use of another species of *like* as a replacement of the verb *say:* "I'm like, 'Yeah, it's like totally wicked awesome.'"

Linguists call this second use "quotative," an introduction to direct speech.

Professor Mark Hale, of the Harvard University Department of Linguistics, says of these speech markers: "This is national in scope. It is not idiosyncratic in any particular part of the country. But it is observed most often among younger people, usually younger than twenty-five."

As a trained linguist, I am fascinated by all change in language, and I don't rush to judgment. The burgeoning of *like* in American discourse appears to be a verbal tic in the linguistic mold of "uh" and "you know." It offers the speaker's thoughts an opportunity to catch up with his or her onrushing sentences or to emphasize important points. Take the statement "I didn't hand in my book report because, like, the dog peed on my Cliff's Notes." Here *like* is an oral mark of crucial punctuation that indicates "important information ahead."

According to Professor Hale, increasing numbers of speakers press into service *go* and *like* for *say* as a badge of identification that proclaims, "I am a member of a certain generation and speech community."

Hmm. My professional rule of thumb is that all linguistic change is neither good nor bad but thinking makes it so. Still, the promiscuous employment of *like* and *go* stirs my concern about the state of our English language. To most of us, *like* is a preposition that means that something is similar to something else but is not the idea or thing itself. Thus, dusting statements with a word of approximation seems to me to encourage half thoughts. I fret that the permeating influence of *like* makes imprecision the norm and keeps both speakers and listeners from coming to grips with the thoughts behind the words. "I'm like a supporter of human rights" lacks the commitment of "I support human rights" because *like* leads off a simile of general likeness, not a literal statement.

I believe that it is not a coincidence that the quotative *like*, just as introductions to quoted speech, has accompanied the burgeoning of *like* as a rhetorical qualifier. I sense a fear of commitment both to direct thought and to the act of communicating—saying and asserting one's observations and opinions. Whenever I hear a young person— or, as is increasingly the case, an older person—declare "She's, like, 'I'm like totally committed to human rights,'" I want to say (not *I'm like*), "Is she really committed? Did she really mean what she said?"

"Language is the Rubicon that divides man from beast," declared the philologist Max Muller. The boundary between our species and the others on this planet that run and fly and creep and swim is the language line. To blur that line by replacing verbs of speaking with verbs of simile is to deny the very act that defines our kind.

I'm like it's totally uncool.

THE GLAMOUR
OF GRAMMAR

Conan the
Grammarian

The owner of a small zoo lost two of his prize animal attractions in a fire. To order another pair, he wrote a letter to a zoological supply company: "Dear Sirs: Please send me two mongooses."

That didn't sound quite right, so he began again with "Dear Sirs: Please send me two mongeese."

Still not sure of that plural either, he made this third attempt: "Dear Sirs: Please send me a mongoose. And, while you're at it, please send me another mongoose."

Many people throughout our land are like the zoo owner, unsure about their usage and fearful of public embarrassment. These needy souls often call on me to make Solomonic judgments about word choice and sentence structure. Sometimes their conceptions of grammar and usage bring to my mind the image of another animal.

In colleges and universities, students from time to time lead a cow upstairs and into an administrator's office. The prank is popular because while you can lead a cow upstairs, you can't lead it downstairs. I know a number of cows like this. They're the bogus usage rules that self-appointed grammarians herd into our national consciousness. It isn't long before we can't get them—the pundits and their rules—out.

One of the most hefty and intractable bovines is the injunction against using of a preposition to end a sentence. The rule banishing terminal prepositions from educated discourse was invented by the late-seventeenth-century British critic and poet John Dryden, who reasoned that *preposito* in Latin means something that "comes before" and that prepositions in Latin never appear at the end of a sentence. Dryden even went so far as to reedit his own works in order to remove the offending construction. A bevy of prescriptive grammarians have been preaching the dogma ever since.

Unfortunately, Dryden neglected to consider two crucial points. First, the rules of Latin don't always apply to English. There exist vast differences between the two languages in their manner of connecting verbs and prepositions. Latin is a language of cases, English a language of word order. In Latin, it is physically impossible for a preposition to appear at the end of a sentence. Second, the greatest writers in English, before and after the time of Dryden, have freely ended sentences with prepositions. Why? Because the construction is a natural and graceful part of our English idiom. Here are a few examples from the masters:

- Fly to others that we know not of.—*William Shakespeare*
- We are such stuff/As dreams are made on.—*William Shakespeare*
- Houses are built to live in, not to look on.—*Francis Bacon*
- What a fine conformity would it starch us all into.—*John Milton*
- . . . soil good to be born on, good to live on, good to die for and to be buried in.—*James Russell Lowell*
- All words are pegs to hang ideas on.—*Henry Ward Beecher*

The final preposition is one of the glories of the English language. If we shackle its idioms and muffle its music with false rules, we diminish the power of our language. If we rewrite the quotations above to conform to Dryden's edict, the natural beauty of our prose and verse is forced to bow before a stiff mandarin code of structure. "Fly to others of whom we know not"; "All words are pegs upon which to hang ideas." Now the statements are artificial—people simply don't talk like that—and, in most cases, wordier.

The most widely circulated tale of the terminal preposition involves Sir Winston Churchill, one of the greatest of all English prose stylists. As the story goes, an officious editor had the audacity to "correct" a proof of Churchill's memoirs by revising a sentence that ended with the outlawed preposition. Sir Winston hurled back at the editor a memorable rebuttal: "This is the sort of errant pedantry up with which I shall not put!"

A variation on this story concerns a newspaper columnist who responded snappily to the accusation that he was uncouthly violating the terminal preposition "rule": "What do you take me for? A chap who doesn't know how to make full use of all the easy variety the English language is capable of? Don't you know that ending a sentence with a preposition is an idiom many famous writers are fond of? They realize it's a colloquialism a skillful writer can do a great deal with. Certainly it's a linguistic device you ought to read about."

For the punster there's the setup joke about the prisoner who asks a female guard to marry him on the condition that she help him escape. This is a man attempting to use a proposition to end a sentence with.

Then there's the one about the little boy who has just gone to bed when his father comes into the room carrying a book about Australia. Surprised, the boy asks: "What did you bring that book that I didn't want to be read to out of from about Down Under up for?"

Now that's a sentence out of which you can get a lot.

My favorite of all terminal preposition stories involves a boy attending public school and one attending private school who end up sitting next to each other in an airplane. To be friendly, the public schooler turns to the preppie and asks, "What school are you at?"

The preppie looks down his aquiline nose at the public school student and comments, "I happen to attend an institution at which we are taught to know better than to conclude sentences with prepositions."

The boy at public school pauses for a moment and then says: "All right, then. What school are you at, dingbat!" (In other versions of this joke, the last word is saltier than *dingbat*.)

Joining the preposition rule in the rogues' gallery of usage enormities is the split infinitive. "Many years ago, when I was a junior in Thornton Academy in Saco, Maine, I was instructed never, under pain of sin, to split an infinitive," wrote one of my column readers. Note the expression "under pain of sin." It speaks of the priestly power of the English teacher to interpret the verbal nature of the universe and to bring down from some kind of Mount Sinai commandments for the moral and ethical use of the Word.

A split infinitive ("to better understand," "to always disagree") occurs when an adverb or adverbial construction is placed between *to* and a verb. In a famous *New Yorker* cartoon, we see Captain Bligh sailing away from the *Bounty* in a rowboat and shouting, "So, Mr. Christian! You propose to unceremoniously cast me adrift?" The caption beneath the drawing reads: "The crew can no longer tolerate Captain Bligh's ruthless splitting of infinitives."

When infinitives are cleft, some schoolmarms, regardless of sex or actual profession, become exercised. Once again we confront the triumph of mandarin decree over reality, of mummified code over usage that actually inhales and exhales—another passionate effort by the absolutists to protect the language from the very people who speak it.

No reputable authority on usage, either in England or in the United States, bans the split infinitive. Major writers—Phillip Sidney, John Donne, Samuel Johnson, Samuel Coleridge, Emily Brontë, Matthew Arnold, Thomas Hardy, Benjamin Franklin, Abraham Lincoln, Oliver Wendell Holmes, Henry James, and Willa Cather (to name a dozen out of thousands)—have been blithely splitting infinitives ever since the early fourteenth century. Thus, when I counsel my readers and listeners to relax about splitting infinitives, I am not, to slightly paraphrase *Star Trek,* telling them to boldly go where no one has gone before. Several studies of modern literary and journalistic writing reveal that a majority of newspaper and magazine editors would accept a sentence using the words "to instantly trace" and that the infinitive is cleft in 19.8 percent of all instances where an adverb appears.

The prohibition of that practice was created in 1762 out of whole cloth by one Robert Lowth, an Anglican bishop and self-appointed grammarian. Like Dryden's anti-terminal-preposition rule, Lowth's anti-infinitive-splitting injunction is founded on models in the classical tongues. But there is no precedent in these languages for condemning the split infinitive because in Greek and Latin (and all the other romance languages) the infinitive (*videre, hablar,* etc.) is a single word that is impossible to sever.

Like Winston Churchill, writers George Bernard Shaw and James Thurber had been stylistically hassled by certain know-it-alls once too often. Shaw struck back in a letter to the *Times* of London: "There is a busybody on your staff who devotes a lot of time to chasing split infinitives. I call for the immediate dismissal of this pedant. It is of no consequence whether he decides to go quickly or to quickly go or quickly to go. The important thing is that he should go at once." With typical precision, concision, and incision, Thurber wrote to a meddlesome editor, "When I split an infinitive, it is going to damn well stay split!"

I'm pleased to announce that a closely guarded secret can now be revealed. Working in a remote area of a top-secret grammar complex, a team of linguistic scientists has succeeded in splitting the infinitive. They placed a stockpile of fissionable gerunds and radioactive participles, encased in leaden clichés to prevent con-fusion, in a machine of their own invention called the infinitron. The effect of the bombardment is to dissociate the word *to* from its main verb until at length an adverb splits an infinitive and is glowingly ejected from the infinitron. But not to worry. The only explosions emanate from Bishop Robert Lowth and his spiritual progeny—those whom Henry W. Fowler, in his dictionary of *Modern English Usage,* describes as people who "betray by their practice that their aversion to the split infinitive springs not from instinctive good taste, but from the tame acceptance of the misinterpreted opinions of others."

Why is the alleged syntactical sin of splitting infinitives committed with such frequency? Primarily because in modern English adjectives and adverbs are usually placed directly before the words they modify, as in "She successfully completed the course." The same people who thunder against adverbs plunked down in the middle of infinitives remain strangely silent about other split expressions: "She has successfully completed the course" (split verb phrase), "She boasted of successfully completing the course" (split prepositional phrase), "It is better to have loved and lost than never to have loved at all" (infinitive split by helping verb). We hear no objections to such sentences because in English it is perfectly natural to place adverbial modifiers before verbs, including infinitive verbs.

I do not advocate that you go about splitting infinitives promiscuously and artlessly. But there is no point in mangling a sentence just to avoid a split infinitive. Good writers occasionally employ the construction to gain emphasis, to attain the most natural and effective word order, and to avoid ambiguity. How would you gracefully rewrite these split-infinitive sentences from recent newspapers?: "By a 5–4 majority, the court voted to permit states to severely restrict women's rights to choose." "It took 33 seasons for Kansas to get back to number one. It took the Jayhawks one game to almost blow it," "The Red Sox shut out the Yankees 6–0 yesterday to all but clinch the American League East division title." And this last one, which shows up on my computer screen whenever I jettison a file: "Are you sure that you want to permanently delete the selected file(s)?" In my view and to my ear, you wouldn't want to revise these constructions; they are already clear and readable.

It is indeed acceptable practice to sometimes split an infinitive. If infinitive splitting makes available just the shade of meaning you desire or if avoiding the separation creates a confusing ambiguity or patent artificiality, you are entitled to happily go ahead and split!

The injunctions against terminal prepositions and cleft infinitives are among the most bulky and balky of the bovines, but smaller and equally immovable critters crowd in: "*Got* is always an uncouth word." "Your work can't be done; it must be finished. That's because meat is done, not work." "A kid is a goat, not a child." "Cattle are raised; children are reared." "Human beings lie on something; inanimate objects lay there." "Never begin a sentence with a coordinating conjunction, such as *and* and *but*." "*None* must always take a singular verb." You get the idea. Dozens of syntactical sins squeak like chalk across the blackboard of so many sensibilities. Yet such proclamations exist as sheer rumor and gossip. They are never enshrined in reputable usage manuals.

From 1954 to 1972, the airwaves were filled with a little jingle that twanged, "Winston tastes good like a cigarette should." English teachers and other word-watchers raised such a fuss about the use of *like* in the song that the publicity was worth millions to the Winston people. So the cigarette hucksters came back with a second campaign: "What do you want—good grammar or good taste?"

My answer to that question is that the use of *like* in the Winston commercial is both good grammar (really, good usage) *and* in good taste.

Among prescriptive grammarians the prevailing rule is that we may use *like* or *as* as a preposition joining a noun—*cleans like a white tornado, blind as a bat*—but we must not use *like* as a conjunction that introduces an adverb clause: The son-of-Winston commercial slogan *Nobody can do it like McDonald's can* is unacceptable because the sentence doesn't sound good like a conjunction should.

Even princes have been royally reprimanded for violating this admonition. Back in the nineteenth century the poet laureate Alfred, Lord Tennyson told the linguist F. J. Furnivall, "It's a modern vulgarism that I have seen grow up within the last thirty years; and when Prince Albert used it in my drawing room, I pulled him up for it, in the presence of the Queen, and told him he never ought to use it again." Tennyson's adamancy about the "rule" is preserved by the panel for the *Harper Dictionary of Contemporary Usage.* These 166 distinguished language experts recently condemned the use of *like* as a conjunction 72–28 percent in casual speech and 88–12 percent in writing.

Cheeky as it may appear, I take issue with the lineup of linguistic luminaries, ranging from Isaac Asimov to William Zinsser. Any open-minded, open-eared observer of the living English language cannot fail to notice that tens of everyday expressions employ *like* as a subordinating conjunction. Fill in the following blanks:

- He tells it _____ it is.
- She ate _____ there was no tomorrow.
- If you knew Suzie _____ I know Suzie . . .
- They make the food here just _____ my mother used to.

And what about *Winston tastes good _____ a cigarette should* and *Nobody can do it _____ McDonald's can?* I am confident that, despite the fact that each blank kicks off an adverb clause, most native English speakers would naturally supply *like.* If I'm wrong, then I guess I don't know my *as* from a hole in the ground.

Oh, yes. If, throughout this screed, you have been wondering whether the zoo owner should have written *mongooses* or *mongeese,* the answer is *mongooses. Goose*, from the Old English *gos*, and *mongoose,* from the Hindi *magus*, are etymologically unrelated. While the plural of *goose* is *geese,* the preferred plural of *mongoose* is *mongooses.* Like most native or experienced users of the English language, the fellow got it right the first time.

Laying Down the Law — Without Lying Down on the Job

Among the dozens of troublesome verb twins, such as *affect/ effect* and *imply/infer*, that can bedevil us, *lie* and *lay* are the most frequently confused pair in the English language. Stealthily, they lie in wait ready to lay confusion and embarrassment upon us.

Here's the problem: *Lie* is a strong, irregular verb that conjugates *lie-lay-lain*. *Lay* is a weak, regular verb that conjugates *lay-laid-laid*. Because *lay* is both the present tense of *to lay* and the past tense of *to lie* and because the weak, regular verb pattern has become dominant in English, many speakers and writers use *lay,* as in "I like to lay in my hammock" (quite a trick!), when they should use *lie*.

The most useful way to sort out *lie* and *lay* is to bear in mind that *lie* is an intransitive verb that means "to repose," while *lay* is usually a transitive verb that means "to put." *Lay* almost always takes an object, *lie* never. Something must be laid, and nothing can be lied. First comes the laying. Then comes the lying.

Or try visualizing this cartoon: Two hens are pictured side by side in their nests. One is sitting on an egg, and she is labeled LAYING; the other is flat on her back and labeled LYING. Sorry for the fowl language, but I always talk turkey without turning chicken!

In another bestial cartoon, a man says to his dog, "Lay down!" and the dog rolls over on its back. Then the master says, "Speak!"— and the dog says, "It's *lie.*"

We can find additional reinforcement in real life for the proper usage of *lie* and *lay*:

The *Toronto Globe and Mail* reported the story of an aged gentleman still sharp of mind and usage: "At 104, when he collapsed during a round of golf, his wife said, 'Oh George. Do you want to lay there a minute?' He opened his eyes and said, '*Lie* there,' before passing out again."

Mary Dillon, of Cumberland Center, Maine, writes: "My friend Beth is a high-school English teacher who lives with her friend Sam, an intelligent Golden Retriever. One day, Beth's mother was riding in the backseat of the car with Sam, who insisted on leaning on Mother. Mother told Sam to 'lay down and behave.' No action. Mother repeated, 'Lay down, Sam.' Still no response. Beth turned and commanded, 'Lie down, Sam,' and down he went. He is after all, the companion of an English teacher."

It's been more than a decade since the Enron scandal broke on the corporate horizon. Here's a little ditty I've written about the company that made an End Run around business ethics, led by its former CEO, the late Ken Lay:

TAKE THE MONEY ENRON

The difference between "lie" and "lay"
Has fallen into deep decay.
But now we know from Enron's shame
That Lay and "lie" are just the same

Sex and the Singular Pronoun

You're sitting at a table and after a long period of time elapses, someone finally brings the food. Why are they called the "waiter"?

I've used this quip dozens of times in my talks and asked the audience if anyone has been offended by any grammatical atrocity I have uttered. Almost no one raises their hand.

Yet some purists grow apoplectic about the use of the pronoun *they* to refer to indefinite pronouns, such as *anyone, each,* and *everybody,* or with singular nouns, as you've just experienced (without trauma, I reckon) twice in the previous two paragraphs. Why is this usage ubiquitous? One reason is that we have been doing it for centuries, all the way back to Middle English. It's been more than six hundred years (1387) since Geoffrey Chaucer wrote, in *The Canterbury Tales,* "And whoso findeth hym out of swich blame,/They wol come up. . . ."

It was not until the eighteenth century that *they* in its third-person singular role was disparaged. That's when such grammarians as Robert Lowth (yes, he of the Anti-Split-Infinitive League) and Lindley Murray decreed that indefinite pronouns are singular. The reasons for this linguistic holding were more cultural than structural. In 1746, for example, John Kirkby's *Eighty Eight Grammatical Rules* included as rule number twenty one that "the male gender is more comprehensive than the female."

Thus we confront the matter of sex and the singular pronoun. While all other pronouns avoid reference to gender, the third-person-singular pronouns in English—*he* and *she*—are gender-specific. We are not fully comfortable with the male chauvinist "Each student should underline in his textbooks so that he can achieve his fullest academic potential" or the clunky "Each student should underline in his or her textbooks so that he or she can achieve his or her fullest academic potential." *They* has long been a graceful solution to the most nettlesome problem in sexist language—the generic masculine pronoun—and to the grammatical stutter engendered by dancing back and forth between the sexes: "Each student should underline in their textbooks so that they can achieve their fullest academic potential."

They has been moving toward singular senses, in the manner of *you*, which can function both singularly and plurally. That's the way we do it—and by *we* I mean we caring and careful speakers and writers. We've been doing it for centuries, and we're doing it today:

- Everyone attended the party, and they had a rockin' time.
- If somebody wants to cut class, we can't stop them.
- The cellular customer you have called has turned off their phone.
- We are required by law to post the pharmacy's number on the medication vial in case the customer has questions about their drug.

The astronomer Galileo Galilei was branded a heretic because he insisted that the earth was not the center of the universe but, in fact, revolved around the sun. Despite his perilous status, Galileo urged others to conduct objective experiments so that they could see the truth for themselves.

Gentle reader, please open your ears and eyes. Listen and look for statements that contain an indefinite pronoun or a singular noun, and hear and see what pronoun follows. In almost every case, that pronoun will be a form of *they*. We do that because the device is historically tested. We do that because it is more graceful than "he or she." And we do that because it avoids making a minority of us the linguistic norm and a majority of us a linguistic afterthought.

An Open Letter
to Ann Landers

Having read the first three chapters in this cluster of *Lederer on Language*, you must be thinking that I am a flaming permissivist who adopts as a household pet any new use of English that crawls out of the language wordwork. But in truth, I constantly fight the good fight to maintain precise differences between the likes of *less* and *fewer* and *I, me,* and *myself.* These are useful distinctions to which the majority of educated speakers and writers continue to adhere. Words are themselves ideas pulsing with particular recognitions and energies that enlarge and quicken life. Blur shades of meaning in language and you blur shades of thinking.

Shortly before Ann Landers' death, a reader wrote to the advice columnist lamenting the parlous state of current usage. In the letter, ENGLISH MAJOR IN OHIO complained of the misuse of the apostrophe to indicate a plural, as in a store sign advertising *Banana's,* and the apostrophe catastrophe of *it's,* used as a possessive pronoun rather than a contraction, as in "A great nation respects it's heritage."

Here, verbatim, is Ann Landers' reply to her concerned reader's complaint:

DEAR ENGLISH MAJOR: You are a purist, a dying breed, and I share your pain. Unfortunately, when people see a word misused or misspelled time after time, they become accustomed to it. Thanks to my readers, I've seen grateful misspelled so many ways, I'm not sure what is right anymore. You ask what can be done about the mistakes we see in print. The answer is, "Very little."

I immediately responded to Ann Landers' response and, although I did not send my letter to her, I share with you, gentle reader, my ungentle polemic:

DEAR ANN LANDERS: Knowing that you are a widely read and respected columnist who from time to time prints letters from readers about the abuse of language, I am surprised by and disappointed in your answer to "English Major in Ohio."

I am aware that English is a living language. Like a tree, language sheds its leaves and grows new ones so that it may live on. But to recognize the reality of and the need for change does not mean that we must accept the mindless permissiveness that pervades the use of English in our society.

Correct usage is written on the sand. The operative words here are *written* and *sand*. It may be that the sand will one day blow away or erode, but at any given moment the sand exists and so does the code of standard discourse.

I was graduated from high school was once the educated idiom; nowadays *I graduated from high school* is not only acceptable, but more appropriate. Many of us speak and write, *I graduated high school,* but that construction is not yet written on the sand of standard usage. *Due to* is loudly knocking on the door of the house once occupied by *because of* and, for most standard speakers and writers what was once almost universally called a lectern (from the Latin "to read") has transmogrified into a podium (from Greek, "foot").

But the differences between *Bananas* and *Banana's* and between *its* and *it's* are not the windy suspirations of what you call a purist; these differences are aspects of basic literacy. To announce to your gazillions of readers that we should shrug our collective shoulders at widespread usage errors because people become "accustomed to" them and that "very little" can be done about such atrocities is to do a disservice to the English language and those who speak and write it.

There are those who contend, "Who cares how you say or write something, as long as people understand you?" This is like saying, "Who cares what clothing you wear, as long as it keeps you warm and covers your nakedness?" But clothing does more than provide warmth and cover, just as language does more than transfer ideas. The sensible man and woman knows when to wear a business suit and when to wear a T-shirt and shorts, when to wear a tuxedo and when to wear a flannel shirt and dungarees. Both clothing and language make statements about the wearer and the user.

And the verbal choices we make can affect meaning. Anyone who strives to speak and write standard English should know the difference between *its* and *it's* because that choice my powerfully affect (not *effect,* although many writers misuse that word) the meaning of a statement, as well as the impression the writer communicates.

In the following sentences, which dog has the upper paw?: (1) A clever dog knows its master. (2) A clever dog knows it's master. The answer, of course, is the second sentence, because it means "A clever dog knows it is master." The use of the apostrophe makes a crucial difference in the meaning conveyed. Moreover, such distinctions have an effect (not *affect*) on the way others view the speaker or writer. I believe that people who call themselves *relators* sell fewer houses than will *Realtors*—and that the store that advertises *Banana's* will not sell as many bananas as the one that goes *bananas.*

Centuries ago, Confucius observed, "If language is not correct, then what is said is not what is meant; if what is said is not what is meant, then what must be done remains undone; if this remains undone, morals and art will deteriorate; if justice goes astray, the people will stand about in helpless confusion. Hence, there must be no arbitrariness in what is said. This matters above everything."

I side with Confucius against the kind of confusion in language that your dismissive and permissive statement engenders. Please reconsider what you wrote to that caring and careful English major in Ohio. And please don't tell us that you, who proffers opinions that change lives, can no longer distinguish *grateful* from *gratefull* from *greatful.*

—ENGLISH LOVER IN SAN DIEGO

SPELLBOUND

Under a Spell

Forskor and sevn yeerz agoe our faadherz braut forth on dhis kontinent a nue naeshun, konseevd in liberti, and dedikated to the propozishun dhat aul men are kreeaeted eekwal.

You've just read the first sentence of Abraham Lincoln's Gettysburg Address recast in the simplified spelling system proposed by Godfrey Dewey. Dr. Dewey is not the only man of good will who has proposed a significant overhaul of our "system" of English spelling. Way back in 1200, the Augustinian monk Orm developed a phonetic spelling system, and in succeeding centuries Orm's lead was followed by such luminaries as Benjamin Franklin, Theodore Roosevelt, George Bernard Shaw, and Upton Sinclair.

In *The Devil's Dictionary,* Ambrose Bierce defines orthography as "the science of spelling by the eye instead of the ear. Advocated with more heat than light by the outmates of every asylum for the insane." "English spelling," declares linguist Mario Pei, "is the world's most awesome mess," while Edward Rondthaler, the inventor of the Soundspel System, labels spelling "a sort of graphic stutter we've tolerated for generations."

Nowhere is the chasm that stretches between phonology (the way we say words) and orthography (the way we spell them) better illustrated than in this eye-popping ditty about the demonic letter combination *-ough:*

Tough Stough

The wind was rough.
The cold was grough.
She kept her hands
Inside her mough.

And even though
She loved the snough,
The weather was
A heartless fough.

It chilled her through.
Her lips turned blough.
The frigid flakes
They blough and flough.

They shook each bough,
And she saw hough
The animals froze—
Each cough and sough.

While at their trough,
Just drinking brough,
Were frozen fast
Each slough and mough.

It made her hiccough—
Worse than a sticcough.
She drank hot cocoa
For an instant piccough.

If the road to language heaven is paved with good intentions, why haven't we Americans responded to the succession of well-intentioned spelling reforms proposed by linguists, clerics, writers, statesmen, and presidents? Because, as in most matters linguistic, simplified spelling is no simple matter.

For one thing, spelling reform would plunder the richness of homophones in the English language. *Rain, rein,* and *reign* were once pronounced differently, but time has made them sound alike. *Knight* was a logical spelling in Chaucer's day, when the *k, n,* and *gh* were distinctly sounded. Today its pronunciation matches that of *night.* In Milton's time, *colonel* was spoken with all three syllables. Now it sounds the same as *kernel.* Thus, the seemingly bizarre spellings that the reformers would excise are actually an aid to differentiation in writing. Think, for example, of the havoc that would be wreaked by spelling the antonyms *raise* and *raze* identically.

So-called simplified spelling turns out to be a snare and a delusion of false simplicity. Instituting such reforms would generate a "big bang" effect, blowing apart words that are currently related. Like the builders of the Tower of Babel, lexical neighbors such as *nature* and *natural* would, as *naechur* and *nachurul,* be divorced and dispersed to separate parts of the dictionary. The same fate would be visited upon conversion pairs such as *record* (noun) and *record* (verb) and *progress* (noun) and *progress* (verb), and our streamlined pattern of noun and verb endings would grow needlessly complex. *Cats* and *dogs* would be transmuted into *kats* and *daugz, walks* and *runs* into *waulks* and *runz,* and *Pat's* and *Ted's* into *Pat's* and *Ted'z.*

Such transformations raise the specter of losing the rich etymological history that current spelling generally preserves. We cannot deny that *seyekaalogee, Wenzdae,* and *troosoe* are accurate visualizations of the sounds they represent. But do we really want to banish the Greekness from *psychology* (from the Greek goddess Psyche), the Scandinavianness from *Wednesday* (from the Norse god Woden), and the romantic Frenchness from *trousseau?*

English is the most hospitable and democratic language that has ever existed. It has welcomed into its vocabulary words from tens of other languages and dialects, far and near, ancient and modern. As Carl Sandburg once observed, "The English language hasn't got where it is by being pure." As James D. Nicoll has quipped, "The problem with defending the purity of English is that English is as pure as a cribhouse whore. We don't just borrow words. On occasion, English has pursued other languages down alleyways to beat them unconscious and rifle their pockets for new vocabulary." Purifying our spelling system would obscure our long history of exuberant borrowing.

A perhaps more telling fret in the armor of simplified spelling is that even its most ardent adherents acknowledge that many words, such as *shejl* and *skejl,* are pronounced differently in the United Kingdom and the United States, necessitating divergent spellings of the same words. Moreover, when we acknowledge the existence of Irish English, Scottish English, Welsh English, Australian English, West Indian English, and all the other world Englishes, we must wonder how many variant spellings we must live with.

Compounding the problem is that pronunciation varies widely in different parts of the same country, a reality that leads us to ask this crucial question: if we are going to embrace an exact phonetic representation of pronunciation, *whose* pronunciation is to be represented? For many Londoners, the *raen* in *Spaen* falls *maenlee* on the *plaen*, but for Eliza Doolittle and many of her cockney and Australian cousins the *rine* in *Spine* falls *minelee* on the *pline.* How will reformers decide which spellings shall prevail?

In the Middle Atlantic states, whence I hail, *cot* and *caught* are sounded distinctly as *kaat* and *kaut.* In New Hampshire, to which I moved, I often heard *kaat* for both words. Not far to my south, many Bostonians say *kaut* for both words. I say *gurl,* in Brooklyn they say *goil* (as in the charmingly reversed "The *oil* bought some *earl*"), and farther south and west they say *gal* and *gurrel.* Because our present system of spelling is as much hieroglyphic as it is phonetic, speakers of English can gaze upon *rain, Spain, mainly, plain, cot, caught,* and *girl* and pronounce the words in their own richly diverse ways.

Even if our spelling were altered by edict, a feat that has never been accomplished in a predominantly literate country, pronunciation would continue to change. As Samuel Johnson proclaimed, "Sounds are too volatile and subtle for legal restraints; to enchain syllables, and to lash the wind, are equally undertakings of pride." No surprise, then, that the good Doctor went on to point out that spelling reformers would be taking "that for a model which is changing while they apply it." The phoneticizing process of spelling reform would itself have to be reformed every fifty or hundred years.

Errors in spelling are the most conspicuous of all defects in written English. Even with the ubiquitousness of spell-checkers, business executives complain about the unchecked and unbridled orthography their employees generate. As a business guru once advised: "A burro is an ass. A burrow is a hole in the ground. As a writer, you are expected to know the difference."

Now gaze upon one hundred words that people in business most frequently misspell. Lurking in the lineup are very probably words that you fear and loathe. Look over the list carefully, and then circle each word that you find to be spelled incorrectly. Then compare your total with the one you find in "Answers to Games and Quizzes."

1. absence
2. accessible
3. accommodate
4. accumulate
5. achieve
6. administration
7. advantageous
8. aggressive
9. analyze
10. appearance
11. apparent
12. appropriate
13. argument
14. background
15. bankruptcy
16. basically
17. before
18. beginning
19. believe
20. benefit
21. business
22. calendar
23. category
24. character
25. committee
26. controversial
27. corroborate
28. definitely
29. dependent
30. description
31. develop
32. dilemma
33. disappear
34. disappoint
35. dissipate
36. effect
37. eligible
38. embarrassing
39. environment
40. exaggerate
41. exercise
42. existence
43. experience
44. finally
45. flexible
46. friend
47. forgo
48. forty
49. gauge
50. harass
51. imitate
52. immediately
53. independent
54. interest
55. judgment
56. liaison
57. license
58. mediocre
59. millennium
60. minuscule
61. necessary
62. negligence
63. negotiable
64. noticeable
65. occasion
66. occurrence
67. omission
68. parallel
69. perseverance
70. piece
71. precede
72. privilege
73. proceed
74. publicly
75. questionnaire
76. receive

77. recommend
78. rescind
79. relieve
80. renown
81. repetition
82. rhythm
83. ridiculous
84. salable
85. secretary
86. seize
87. sentence
88. separate

89. sincerely
90. skillful
91. successful
92. supersede
93. surprise
94. their
95. threshold
96. through
97. tomorrow
98. truly
99. whether
100. writing

I Before *E*,
Except . . . ?

At the William Cullen Bryant School, in West Philadelphia, my seventh-grade English teacher, Mrs. Huckins, had blue hair, wore wire-rimmed glasses and a paisley smock, and kept an avocado seed in a glass vase on the radiator. I wish that everyone could have a Mrs. Huckins in language arts, for she was the light-bearing mentor who wrought order from orthographic chaos, the lawgiver who taught me the basic spelling rules: how to drop the *y* and add *ie* in words such as *babies* and *studied,* how to double the final consonant in words such as *stopping* and *occurrence,* and, of course, "*i* before *e,* except after *c.*" Alas, though, as I gradually attained the age of the sere and yellow leaf, I came to realize that the last formula did not really work. Granted that an occasional exception may prove a rule, but this rule, honored as much in the breach as in the observance, has so many exceptions that the exceptions bury the rule.

To begin with, the most famous of all spelling jingles has a small amendment tacked on:

> *I* before *e,*
> Except after *c,*
> Unless sounded as *a,*
> As in *neighbor* and *weigh.*

The last two lines suggest aberrations such as *beige, deign, eight, feign, feint, geisha, heinous, heir, inveigh, inveigle, lei, neigh, neighbor, reign, rein, reindeer, skein, sleigh, their, veil, vein, weigh,* and *weight.* That makes twenty-three exceptions to the *i*-before-*e* dictum already.

Another batch of mutants consists of words in which both the *e* and the *i* are sounded: *absenteeism, agreeing, albeit, atheist, being, contemporaneity, decreeing, dyeing, fleeing, freeing, guaranteeing, pedigreeing, plebeian, reimburse, reincarnate, reinfect, reinforce, reinstate, reintegrate, reinterpret, reinvent, reinvest, reissue, reiterate, seeing, simultaneity, spontaneity, teeing,* and *treeing*. This raises the subtotal of exceptions to fifty-two, one for each week of the year.

It doesn't take a genius to realize that the *i* before *e* rule doesn't work for the names of many people and places: "Eugene *O'Neill* and Dwight D. *Eisenhower* drank 35-degree-*Fahrenheit Budweiser* and *Rheingold* in *Anaheim* and *Leicester*." We could add a long scroll of names to the cluster, such as *Stein* and *Weiss,* but we'll be lenient and count all *ei* personal names as one exception and all *ei* place names as another, bumping the subtotal of rule-flouters up to fifty-four.

"Cut the orthographic obfuscation, Lederer," I can hear you thinking. "Your last two categories of *i*- before-*e* violations verge on the bogus."

Very well. Here are thirty-four breaches of the observance that do not involve names, separately pronounced vowels, or a long *a* sound: *caffeine, codeine, counterfeit, eiderdown, either, feisty, foreign, forfeit, heifer, heigh ho, height, heist, herein, kaleidoscope, keister, leisure, neither, nonpareil, obeisance, onomatopoeia, protein, rein, reveille, seismograph, seize, sheikh, sleight, sovereign, stein, surfeit, therein, weir, weird,* and *wherein*.

Having accumulated eighty-eight exceptions to a spelling rule that appears to have been made to be broken, let us now attack the amendment "except after *c*." This little disclaimer works perfectly well for words such as *receive* and *ceiling,* but what about those in which *c* is followed by *ie*?: *agencies, ancient, aristocracies, autocracies, chancier, concierge, conscience, contingencies, currencies, democracies, emergencies, exigencies, fallacies, fancied, financier, glacier, mercies, omniscient, policies, science, society, species, sufficient,* and *tendencies*.

Now have a look at three more words of this type: *deficiencies, efficiencies,* and *proficiencies*. Note that these are all double plays, each shattering the rule twice in adjacent syllables. But we shall remain flexible and count each as only a single violation, bringing the subtotal to 115.

In the same category, if we are to move upward and outward, we shall have to consult a genius, like Albert *Einstein*. Einstein would point out that his surname is another double violation, but, having already counted all personal names as a single exception, we shall not add his. We do note, however, that an Einstein might spout arcane, abstruse words such as *beidellite, corporeity, cuneiform, deice, deictic, deionize, eidolon, femineity, gaseity, greige, hermaphrodeity, heterogeneity, homogeneity, leifite, leister, leitmotif, meiosis, mythopoeic, peiramater, reify, reive, rheic, seity, sulphureity, weibullite, xanthoproteic, zein,* and *zeitgeist* (another double exception). These handy, everyday words raise our subtotal of exceptions to 143, just one away from proving that the most renowned of all spelling aphorisms is (ahem) grossly misleading.

To show how much this rule was made to be broken, I offer a poem that I hope will leave you spellbound:

E-I, I-E—Oh?

There's a rule that's sufficeint, proficeint, efficeint.
For all speceis of spelling in no way deficeint.
While the glaceirs of ignorace icily frown,
This soveriegn rule warms, like a thick iederdown.

On words fiesty and wierd it shines from great hieghts,
Blazes out like a beacon, or skien of ieght lights.
It gives nieghborly guidance, sceintific and fair,
To this nonpariel language to which we are hier.

Now, a few in soceity fiegn to deride
And to forfiet thier anceint and omnisceint guide,
Diegn to worship a diety foriegn and hienous,
Whose counterfiet riegn is certain to pain us.

In our work and our liesure, our agenceis, schools,
Let us all wiegh our consceince, sieze proudly our rules!
It's plebiean to lower our standards. I'll niether
Give in or give up—and I trust you won't iether!

Now that we've reached a total of 143 violations of the *i*-before-*e* rule, can we uncover one more common exception that will bring the count to a satisfying dozen dozen? For the answer we'll have to consult the *Deity*.

Fairly Familiar Phrases

Here's a cluster-closing game to whet your appetite—or (great expectorations!) wet your appetite—for spelling challenges.

The phrases below may be as familiar to you as your old stamping—or is it stomping?—grounds, but when it comes to spelling them, you may be in dire straights—or is it dire straits? Like the cat that ate cheese and then breathed into the mousehole, I'm sure that you're waiting with baited breath—or should that be bated breath?—and chomping (or perhaps champing?) at the bit. May your answers and mine jibe—or maybe jive?—completely so that you don't miss any by a hare's breath—or hare's breadth? or hair's breath? or hair's breadth?

Homophones and sound-alikes can often reek—or is it wreck or wreak?—havoc. In each phrase that follows, choose the preferred spelling.

1. anchors *away/aweigh* 2. to wait with *baited/bated* breath 3. to grin and *bare/bear* it 4. sound *bite/byte* 5. *bloc/block* voting

6. a *ceded/seeded* player 7. *champing/chomping* at the bit 8. a full *complement/compliment* of 9. to strike a responsive *chord/cord* 10. just *deserts/desserts*

10. doesn't *faze/phase* me 12. to have a *flair/flare* for 13. *foul/fowl* weather 14. *hail/hale* and *hardy/hearty* 15. a *hair's/hare's breadth/breath*

16. a seamless *hole/whole* 17. a friend in need is a friend *in deed/indeed* 18. it doesn't *jibe/jive* 19. on the *lam/lamb* 20. to the *manner/manor born/borne*

21. *marshal/martial* law 22. to test one's *medal/meddle/metal/ mettle* 23. *might/mite* and *mane/main* 24. beyond the *pale/pail* 25. to *peak/peek/pique* one's interest

26. *pi/pie* in the sky 27. *pidgin/pigeon* English 28. *plain/plane* geometry 29. to *pore/pour* over an article 30. *praying/preying* mantis

31. a matter of *principal/principle* 32. *rack/wrack* one's brain 33. to give free *rain/reign/rein* 34. *raise/raze Cain/cane* 35. to pay *rapped/ rapt/wrapped* attention

36. with *reckless/wreckless* abandon 37. to *reek/wreak/wreck* havoc 38. *right/rite/write* of passage 39. a *shoe-/shoo-*in 40. to *sic/sick* the dog on someone

41. *sleight/slight* of hand 42. *spit and/spitting* image 43. the old *stamping/stomping* grounds 44. to *stanch/staunch* the flow 45. dire *straights/straits*

46. a *toe-/tow-headed* youth 47. to *toe/tow* the line 48. to swear like a *trooper/trouper* 49. all in *vain/vane/vein* 50. to *wet/whet* one's appetite

GETTING THE
WORD OUT

Writing Is . . .

For me, writing is like throwing a Frisbee.

You can play Frisbee catch with yourself, but it's repetitious and not much fun. Better it is to fling to others, to extend yourself across a distance.

At first, your tossing is awkward and strengthless. But, with time and practice and maturity, you learn to set your body and brain and heart at the proper angles, to grasp with just the right force, and not to choke the missile. You discover how to flick the release so that all things loose and wobbly snap together at just the right moment. You learn to reach out your follow-through hand to the receiver to ensure the straightness and justice of the flight.

And on the just-right days, when the sky is blue and the air pulses with perfect stillness, all points of the Frisbee spin together within their bonded circle—and the object glides on its own whirling, a whirling invisible and inaudible to all others but you.

Like playing Frisbee, writing is a re-creation-al joy. For me, a lot of the fun is knowing that readers out there—you among them—are sharing what I have made. Like a whirling, gliding Frisbee, my work extends me beyond the frail confines of my body.

Thank you for catching me.

How I Write

Ernest Hemingway's first rule for writers was to apply the seat of the pants to the seat of the chair. But not all authors are able to survive with such a simple approach.

Emile Zola pulled the shades and composed by artificial light. Francis Bacon, we are told, knelt each day before creating his greatest works. Martin Luther could not write unless his dog was lying at his feet, while Ben Jonson needed to hear his cat purring.

Marcel Proust sealed out the world by lining the walls of his study with cork. Gertrude Stein and Raymond Carver wrote in their cars, while Edmond Rostand preferred to write in his bathtub. Emily Dickinson hardly ever left her home and garden. Wallace Stevens composed poetry while walking to and from work each day at a Hartford insurance company. Alexander Pope and Jean Racine could not write without first declaiming at the top of their voices. Jack Kerouac began each night of writing by kneeling in prayer and composing by candlelight. Dan Brown rises to write at 4 a.m., seven days a week. As an antidote to the dreaded writer's block, he hangs upside down like a bat until the creative juices begin flowing. Friedrich Schiller started each of his writing sessions by opening the drawer of his desk and breathing in the fumes of the rotten apples he had stashed there.

Some writers have donned and doffed gay apparel. Early in his career, John Cheever wore a business suit as he traveled from his apartment to a room in his basement. Then he hung the suit on a hanger and wrote in his underwear. Jessamyn West wrote in bed without getting dressed, as, from time to time, did Eudora Welty, Edith Wharton, Mark Twain, and Truman Capote. John McPhee worked in his bathrobe and tied its sash to the arms of his chair to keep from even thinking about deserting his writing room.

For stimulation, Honoré de Balzac wrote in a monk's costume and drank at least twenty cups of coffee a day, eventually dying of caffeine poisoning. As his vision failed, James Joyce took to wearing a milkman's uniform when he wrote, believing that its whiteness caught the sunlight and reflected it onto his pages. Victor Hugo went to the opposite lengths to ensure his daily output of words on paper. He gave all his clothes to his servant with orders that they be returned only after he had finished his day's quota.

Compared to such strategies, my daily writing regimen is drearily normal. Perhaps that's because I'm a nonfictionalist—a hunter-gatherer of language who records the sounds that escape from the holes in people's faces, leak from their pens, and luminesce up on their computer screens. I don't drink coffee. Rotten fruit doesn't inspire (literally "breathe into") me. My lifelong, heels-over-head love affair with language is my natural caffeine and fructose.

To be a writer, one must behave as writers behave. They write. And write. And write. The difference between a writer and a wannabe is that a writer is someone who can't not write, while a wannabe says, "One of these days when . . ., then I'll. . . ." Unable not to write, I write almost every day.

A grocer doesn't wait to be inspired to go to the store and a banker to go to the bank. I can't afford the luxury of waiting to be inspired before I go to work. Writing is my job, and it happens to be a job that almost nobody gives up on purpose. I love my job as a writer, so I write. Every day that I can.

Long ago, I discovered that I would never become the Great American Novelist. I stink at cobbling characters, dialogue, episode, and setting. You won't find much of that fictional stuff in my books, unless the story serves the ideas I am trying to communicate. A writer has to find out what kind of writer he or she is, and I somehow got born an English teacher with an ability to illuminate language and literature. In my work, ideas, not characters, are the heroes.

Jean-Jacques Rousseau wrote only in the early morning, Alain-Rene Lesage at midday, and Lord Byron at midnight. Early on, I also discovered that I am more lark than owl—more a morning person than a night person—and certainly not a bat, one who writes through the night. I usually hit the ground punning at around 7:30 a.m., and I'm banging away at the keyboard within an hour.

I write very little on paper, almost everything on my computer. Theodore Sturgeon once wrote, "Nine-tenths of everything is crap." The computer allows me to dump crap into the hard drive without the sense of permanence that handwriting or type on paper used to signify to me. I'm visual and shape my sentences and paragraphs most dexterously on a screen. The computer has not only trebled my output. It has made me a more joyful, liberated, and better writer.

Genetic and environmental roulette has allowed me to work in either a silent or a noisy environment. I'm a speaker as well as a writer, so phone calls and faxes and e-messages chirp and hum and buzz in my writing room, and I often have to answer them during those precious morning hours. That's all right with me. Fictionalists shut the world out. Fictionalists live with their imaginary characters, who get skittish and may flee a noisy room. As I cobble my essays, my readers are my companions, and they will usually stay with me in my writing space through outerworldly alarms and excursions.

Besides, the business of the writing business gives me the privilege of being a writer. In fact, I consider the writing only about half my job. Writers don't make a living writing books. They make a living selling books. After all, I do have to support my writing habit.

My whole life has been an effort to obliterate the distance between who I am and what I do. When you are heels over head in love with what you do, you never work a day. That's me: butt over teakettle in love with being a writer—a job that nobody who works it would give up on purpose.

Plane Talk

Like Billy Pilgrim, in Kurt Vonnegut's *Slaughterhouse Five,* I often become unstuck in time.

While tooting around on a promotional book tour, I suddenly find myself in one o'clock in the morning on a Wednesday, which means that I must have just landed in Los Angeles. I've flown in from Denver, where I did an interview with *The Denver Post* and a signing at a Denver bookstore. That same day I winged my way to Denver from Houston, where I had done some other radio work and book signings. I've flown from New York to Boston to Philadelphia to Washington, D.C., to Atlanta to Milwaukee to Chicago to Houston to Denver, and I'll be winging my way from Los Angeles to San Francisco to Seattle to Vancouver to Winnipeg to Toronto—one day at a time.

Logging so many air miles, I have been frequently exposed to "plane talk," the loopy jargon of the airline industry. Two wrongs don't make a right, but two Wrights did make an airplane, over a century before the initial takeoff of the book you're reading. To learn how flighty and fly-by-the-seat-of-the-pants is our English language, take off with me on a typical tour day:

I wake up in my hotel room for the night, and I take the elevator down to the lobby. I note that the name *elevator* actually describes only half of what the machines do. Something that elevates goes up, so how can an elevator descend?

It does, though, and I get in a shuttle bus that goes back and forth to the airport terminal. Actually, it goes *forth and back,* since you have to go forth before you can go back. And I don't know about you, but that word *terminal* always scares me when it's in an airport.

On the way to the airport, the bus enters rush-hour traffic. Despite the word *hour,* I notice that, in most big cities, rush hour usually lasts more than sixty minutes. The bus gets caught in a big traffic bottleneck. But it's really a *small* traffic bottleneck because the bigger the bottleneck, the more easily the fluid flows through it. Yet you never hear anyone say, "Boy, this morning I got caught in one of the smallest traffic bottlenecks of my life!"

Now that I'm at the (gasp!) terminal, I ask the airline official behind the counter if I am on a nonstop flight. Fortunately, she says that I am not. That's good because I want the flight to stop somewhere. The trouble with nonstop flights is that you never get down.

At any rate, the voice on the public address system announces that it's time to preboard. *Preboard* strikes me as something that people do *before* they board, but I notice that those who are preboarding are actually boarding.

Then it's time for the rest of us to get on the plane. I don't know about you, but I don't get *on* a plane; I get *in* a plane.

As I am about to get in the plane, one of the flight attendants cautions me, "Watch your head." I rotate my cranium in every direction, but I am still unable to watch my head. Trying to watch your head is like trying to bite your teeth.

A little later, the flight attendant assures us that "the aircraft will be in the air momentarily." I know she's thinking that *momentarily* means "in a moment," but I am among the vanishing band of Americans who believe that *momentarily* means "for a moment." The thought of the plane soaring upward "momentarily" does not soothe my soul.

On the flight, I pray that we won't have a near miss. *Near miss,* an expression that has grown up since World War II, logically means a collision. If a mass of metal hurtling through the skies nearly misses another object, I figure it hits it. *Near hit* is the more accurate term, and I hope to avoid one of those, too.

Then I hear a voice on the public address system informing me that "in about twenty minutes we'll be landing in the San Diego area." In the area? How about if we actually land in San Diego, preferably at the airport?

Then comes the most chilling moment of all. The dulcet voice on the airplane intercom announces that we should fasten our seat belts and secure our carry-on bags because we are beginning our "final descent." *Final descent!* Hoo boy, does that sound ominous. I pray that we passengers will live to experience other descents in our lives. No wonder that some people experience fear of flying. What they really feel is fear of crashing!

Incredibly, the aircraft touches down with all of us alive and begins to taxi on the runway. If planes taxi on runways, I wonder, do taxis plane on streets? Now the same voice asks us to keep our seat belts fastened until the aircraft "comes to a complete stop." That reassures me, as I wouldn't want the vehicle to come to "a partial stop," which, of course, would be an oxymoron.

Finally, the vehicle does come to a complete stop, and we are told that we can safely deplane. After that, I'll decab, decar, or debus and enter another hotel. The next morning I'll wake up to face another day of plane talk.

Radio Days

"I love radio people," says Richard Lederer ex-statically. In the hundreds of in-studio and on-the-telephone interviews that I have done with radio broadcasters around the United States and the United Kingdom, I have discovered that the English language is in good mouths with radio people. Almost all the radio folk who have interviewed me have actually read the book we're supposed to be talking about and have been genuinely excited about the material. I have been delighted, but not surprised; words are the stuff that radio is made on, and radio broadcasters earn their livings painting pictures with words.

Thanks to the magic of teleconferencing, often the format for a given show is call-in, and the phones and airwaves crackle with logolepsy. I truly get my audio radiance from my radio audience. When people ask me if I miss teaching, my happy experiences on the radio have led me to answer, "I haven't left teaching." In a less intimate but broader way, I now reach more people in a month than in a lifetime of teaching, especially through my regular appearances on San Diego, Wisconsin, Rochester, San Francisco, Toronto, and Boston public and commercial radio.

At times, the teacher becomes the student, and I learn something new from the callers. Once on "New York and Company," the popular New York public radio call-in show hosted by Leonard Lopate, a listener called wanting to know my opinion of the origin of the phrase *the spitting image.* I offered two possible explanations: One theory maintains that *the spitting image* is derived from "the spirit and image" (the inner and outer likeness) and that in Renaissance English and southern American speech *spirit* became *spi'it*, with the *r* dropped. A second hypothesis proposes that *spitting* really means what it says and that *the spitting image* carries the notion of the off-spring's being "identical even down to the spit" of the parent.

Immediately the WNYC studio switchboard lit up with listeners eager to expound their theories. Quoting idioms from various languages, callers demonstrated that the metaphor is truly salivary. In French, for example, the expression is *C'est son père tout craché.* ("He is his father all spat out.") Great expectorations! For the first time I could be certain that the second explanation of *the spitting image* was the correct one.

While I was doing a show via telephone with host Davis Rankin on KURV, a small station in southwest Texas, a listener called to ask about the origin of the word *malarkey*. I responded that I had consulted many reputable dictionaries about this word, and all had sighed, "origin unknown." A few minutes later a caller named Lynn got on the line to disagree. She claimed that she was descended from an Irish family named Malarkey, in which the men were reputed for their great size and athletic feats. As tall Irish tales about the Malarkeys' prowess spread, *malarkey* came to be a synonym for *blarney,* another word of Irish descent, originating with the Blarney stone, at Blarney Castle, near Cork. Those who are courageous enough to hang by their heels and kiss the stone are rewarded with the gift of persuasive gab.

Who knows? Lynn's explanation could be a bunch of malarkey, or she could know whereof she speaks. If she is right, she has enriched our knowledge of the origins and development of a beguiling English word.

One of my favorite forums for interviews and call-ins is *The Jim Bohannon Show*, on which I've had the great pleasure of appearing several times. Jim is the exuberant and highly verbivorous host of the three-hour talk show that airs from Washington, D.C. *The Jim Bohannon Show* is on a clear channel that reaches almost every state in the USA, and when Jim opens the lines for callers, the in-studio telephone board incandesces. From Maine to California, from Florida to Washington State, one can hear the multifold accents and concerns that reflect a sprawling and diverse nation of speakers. Best of all, Jim doesn't just interview me; he himself enters into the spirit of the wordplay.

Here, just about verbatim and with a minimum of cutting and polishing, is a swatch of call-ins and responses that illustrate just how lively and well is the state of the English language in our states. Jim's opening interview with me has just ended, and we go to the call-in segment of the show:

JB: All right, your turn. Let's go to the phones right now. The number is 703-555-2177. Hello, Portland, Oregon.

Caller: Hi. Why does no word rhyme with *orange?*

RL: It's not true that no word rhymes with *orange.* You see, Jim, there are a number of words that are famous for being unrhymable, and the two most famous are *orange* and *silver.* However, there was a man—I'm not kidding—named Henry Honeychurch Gorringe. He was a naval commander who in the mid-nineteenth century oversaw the transport of Cleopatra's Needle to New York's Central Park. Pouncing on this event, the poet Arthur Guiterman wrote:

> *In Sparkhill buried lies a man of mark*
> *Who brought the Obelisk to Central Park,*
> *Redoubtable Commander H.H. Gorringe,*
> *Whose name supplies the long-sought rhyme for orange.*

Or you can bend the rules of line breaks and sound as Willard Espy did:

> *Four eng-*
> *ineers*
> *Wear orange*
> *brassieres.*

So *orange* is rhymable.

Caller: And I have a pun for you: Why is Daffy Duck so daffy? Because he smokes quack.

RL: Very good. Now, I've got a duck pun for you. Who was the only duck president of the United States, sir?

Caller: Abraham Lincoln?

RL: Pretty close. Mallard Fillmore. You can't duck that one.

JB: And there was the great duck explorer—Francis Drake. Philadelphia, you're on the air.

Caller: What is a thirteen-letter word in which the first eight letters mean "the largest," and the complete word means "the smallest"?

RL: Oh boy, you've got me.

JB: Oh, I know—infinitesimal.

Caller: Correct. You're too good, Jim.

JB: Kansas City is next as we talk with Richard Lederer.

Caller: There was a little country that was chastised by all the other countries because it was a bad little country. The other countries wouldn't throw any commerce the little country's way, so it kept yelling, "O grab me! O grab me!" Well, all the other countries thought that turning the tables was fair play, so here's what they did: "Embargo."

RL: That's a very clever semordnilap, a palindrome that reads backwards. *Embargo* is "O grab me" reversed.

JB: Nashua, New Hampshire, you're on the air.

RL: Woooo, Nashua, one of *my* people.

Caller: Yes, a fellow Granite Stater.

RL: We take nothing for granite there. Go ahead.

Caller: What's the deal between "I could care less" and "I couldn't care less"?

RL: The deal is that logically you couldn't care less. If you say that you could care less, then you care to some extent and are being careless about "care less." But remember, sir, that negatives are very unstable in English, so we say, "Let's see if we can't do it" when we mean, "Let's see if we can do it." Or "I really miss not seeing you" really means "I really miss seeing you."

JB: We go to Houston next, hello.

Caller: I'm a big fan of puns. We use them a lot at work. They're good for cutting the seriousness away from things. One of the little things we do at work. We take a phrase like "the leading edge of technology," and we say, "Bakers are on the kneading edge of technology," "Taxicab drivers are on the fleeting edge of technology," and "Lawyers are on the pleading edge of technology."

JB: And doctors are on the bleeding edge of technology.

RL: Stockbrokers are on the greeding edge of technology.

Caller: And gardeners are on the weeding edge.

RL: Or on the seeding edge.

JB: And very shortly after this show we're going to have an announcer on the reading edge. He's going to update us on the news. Saulte St. Marie, Canada, you're next with Richard Lederer.

Caller: I just wanted to ask Richard a couple of spelling words. What do the letters M-A-C-D-U-F-F spell?

RL: Macduff.

Caller: And what does M-A-C-I-N-T-O-S-H spell?

RL: Macintosh.

Caller: And what does M-A-C-H-I-N-E-R-Y spell?

RL: I don't want to ruin your night, ma'am, but it's *machinery*, not *MacHinery* .

JB: We go to Hamden, Connecticut.

Caller: Heaveno, Jim; heaveno, Richard.

JB: This is a man who does not like to say "hello" because this is a family program. He prefers to say, "heaveno."

Caller: There are three groups of words: *sun* and *fun,* which are similar; *woo* and *wound,* which are opposites; and *toast* and *coast,* which are unrelated. It seems that in a good language words that sound the same should mean the same.

RL: I beg to differ. Language reflects the fearful asymmetry of the human race, and you can't get that kind of logic. In a perfectly logical language, if *pro* and *con* are opposites, then is *congress* the opposite of *progress*? I mean we have a language in which "what's going on?" and "what's coming off?" mean the same thing, while a wise man and a wise guy are opposites, a language in which the third hand on a clock or watch is called the second hand and your nose can run and your feet smell. I'm not looking for logic in language, because human beings, not computers, make language, and we're not logical.

JB: Indianapolis, you're on the air with *The Jim Bohannon Show.*

Caller: Why did they use to name hurricanes with female names? Because otherwise they'd have been him-icanes. The reason I called is I thought you'd get a kick out of this—I can't see, and every once in a while I meet a young lady that I'd like to get acquainted with, and my favorite line is, "Would you like a blind date?"

RL: Very funny. You are sightless, sir?

Caller: Yes, I am. And I have run into—oops, there's another figure of speech—some short women. I'm presently dating a girl who's four foot three, and I told her that it's better to have loved a short girl than never to have loved a tall.

RL: Oooooh, this guy is very good. Have you heard about the blind fellow who takes his seeing eye dog into a store and the man picks up the dog and whirls it around over his head. The shopkeeper asks, "What are you doing?" And the blind man says . . .

Caller: "We're just browsing."

JB: This is Baltimore next.

Caller: Mr. Bohannon, I'd like to ask Mr. Lederer a question about words. There are three words in the English language that end in *g-r-y*. Two of them are *angry* and *hungry*. What is the third?

RL: Thank you for asking that, sir. You have given me a wonderful opportunity to perform a great service to the American people because what you are quoting is one of the most outrageous linguistic hoaxes in this country.

The answer is that there is no answer, at least no satisfactory answer. May I advise anybody who happens on the *angry+hungry+?* poser, which slithered onto the American scene around 1975, to stop wasting time and to move on to a more productive activity, like counting the number of angels on the head of a pin or searching for a way to write the sentence "There are three *twos (to's, too's)* in the English language."

There are at least fifty *-gry* words in addition to *angry* and *hungry,* and every one of them is either a variant spelling, as in *augry* for *augury*, *begry* for *beggary,* and *bewgry* for *buggery,* or ridiculously obscure, as in *anhungry,* an obsolete synonym for *hungry; aggry,* a kind of variegated glass bead much in use in the Gold Coast of West Africa; *puggry,* a Hindu scarf wrapped around the helmet or hat and trailing down the back to keep the hot sun off one's neck; or *gry,* a medieval unit of measurement equaling one-tenth of a line.

A much better puzzle of this type is "Name a common word, besides *tremendous, stupendous,* and *horrendous,* that ends in *-dous.*" Why don't we invite the callers to submit their opinions on this one?

JB: West Palm Beach, Florida, you're next.

Caller: Yes, Mr. Lederer, does a person graduate college or graduate from college?

RL: Or is the person graduated from college? Logically, one is graduated from college since the college confers the degree on the students. That has changed, and educated people are perfectly comfortable with the active-voice "graduate from college." I'd avoid "graduate college." It's awkward and sounds as if the person is doing the graduating of the institution.

JB: Athens, Georgia, you're on the air.

Caller: I have a pun for Mr. Lederer. A member of a New York state family had committed a murder and been electrocuted in the electric chair at Sing Sing. To put the best face on the affair, this man's descendants would say that the man once occupied the chair of Applied Electricity in one of the state's leading institutions.

RL: A wonderful example of a euphemism, calling a spade a heart.

JB: Gaithersburg, Maryland, you're on the air.

Caller: I want to share a true pun opportunity that came up many years ago. I was coordinating a serious business meeting, the attendance of which was supposed to include a gentleman named Cappella, and at the last minute we got a note that Mr. Cappella was unable to attend the meeting. I remarked that the meeting would have to be held a Cappella—and got nothing but cold stares.

RL: Your colleagues are just jealous. As Oscar Levant once said, "A pun is the lowest form of humor, when you don't think of it first."

JB: This is Clackamas, Oregon.

Caller: I've got one thing to ask. I used to tell quite a lot of puns myself, until I learned that there was some danger to it, so I gave them up. My main fear in the afterlife was eternal punnish-ment.

JB: We go to Austin, Texas. Richard Lederer is on with you. Hello.

Caller: Good evening. Did you ever get an answer for the fourth word ending in *-dous?*

JB: No, and thanks for reminding us. OK, *tremendous, stupendous, horrendous*—and . . .

Caller: Hazardous.*

---

* At least thirty-two additional *-dous* words repose in various dictionaries: *apodous, antropodous, blizzardous, cogitabundous, decapodous, frondous, gastropodous, heteropodous, hybridous, iodous, isopodous, jeopardous, lagopodous, lignipodous, molybdous, mucidous, multifidous, nefandous, nodous, octapodous, palladous, paludous, pudendous, repandous, rhodous, sauropodous, staganopodous, tetrapodous, thamphipodous, tylopodous, vanadous,* and *voudous.*

English with a Russian Dressing

At Senate Square in Saint Petersburg, Russia, my wife, Simone, and I gaze upon a magnificent bronze statue of Peter the Great, which faces the Neva River. The czar of czars is mounted on a rearing steed that tramples a writhing serpent. The tableau represents the victory of Russia over Sweden in the Northern War.

Our guide and hostess, Tatyana Vereshkina, observes a small crowd of children swarming up and down the stone wave that forms the base of the massive sculpture. In their enthusiasm, the boys and girls often bump against the snake. Tatyana clucks, "Well, I've never seen that before, children playing on the statue. They're going to do some damage there. And look at the parents just standing about and allowing the kids to run wild. That statue used to be cordoned off. But I guess that's what happens when you get democracy."

It is the middle of 1994, and for eleven days I am visiting and teaching in a number of schools in Saint Petersburg. I have been invited to the city by the Centre for Concerned Teachers and SPELTA (Saint Petersburg English Language Teachers Association) to show how instruction in English can be made more fun. During my stay, I work with students from ten-year-old third graders to twenty-one-year-old university students of philology to the teachers themselves.

Saint Petersburg is a city of striking contrasts. On our way from the airport, we see, amid the rows of white birches, billboards for American products. On Nevsky Prospekt, the Champs Elysees of the city, exquisite eighteenth-century palaces sit next to Baskin-Robbins ice cream shops.

Saint Petersburg struggles to recover its splendor, but for now the capital and jewel of the Russian empire has been badly cracked by the hammer of history. It is a bright, cold day in May, and the clocks are striking thirteen—or fourteen or fifteen, any possible time—because most of the clocks don't work. Heaps of rocks and bricks and tree limbs—all manner of smashed debris—lie everywhere. Most mail doesn't get into or out of Russia. The public dial telephones are battered. The public toilets stink. There are scarcely any trash cans. The ruble lies in rubble, inflating at a 2,000 percent annual rate, sending pensioners into the streets of beg and invoking the specter of the Weimar Republic. Many shops are closed, and rows of temporary kiosks line the streets. Where are the baby carriages? Where are the babies?

During the first day, as I am sitting in the Metro, a drunk sways before me, then pitches forward and crashes into my face. Later that day I find my back pocket slashed. Someone seeking a wallet I wasn't carrying. Welcome to Russia.

Tatyana Vereshkina is an assistant principal and English teacher at School 105, one of the schools where I taught. She shares a treasure chest of compositions and artwork from her 10- to 12-year-olds. All the hues missing from their lives in the city they pour into their drawings, alive and struck through with bursting color. The quality and imagination of their writing made the head swim and the blood sing:

We are looking for an ideal teacher of English. So we decided to place an advertisement in the paper "The Sunday Mirror" saying what qualities the teacher should possess.

First of all, the teacher should be competent. That means that she/he should have advanced knowledge of languages, as well as the skill to manage children. The teacher should also be a pleasant person to deal with—bright and witty.

Besides, the teacher should be not only mentally fit but also physically fit to enjoy playing with children. And the last quality but not the least one—to be patient. Is there any ideal teacher of that kind?

I trust you'll agree that this little essay would earn a solid grade in most of our junior high schools. It happens to have been written by Dmitiri Amahin, a ten-year-old third grader at School 105. Despite severe shortages of books, blackboards, and audiovisual bells and whistles, Russian students certainly do learn their English language. Amid the drab devastation, bankrupt infrastructure, and shards of broken philosophies that haunt Saint Petersburg glows an abiding respect and remarkable passion for English. Russia has more English teachers than the United States has students of Russian. English has long been the most popular foreign language taught in the former Soviet Union and is required for most Russian pupils and students. Typically, pupils start learning English in the first, second, or third grade, studying the language for three hours each week. In the upper levels they increase their English immersion to six hours each week, including Saturday mornings.

The first day I arrive at School 105 I am welcomed by the fifth-grade boys and girls in the Friendship Club. The club adviser, Valentina Frantseva, tells me her story: "I went to school in Kazakhstan, just after the war. My father came home from the front, and I was afraid of him. Then I was afraid of the children in my class. The teachers were so strict that they wouldn't let you go to the bathroom. At that moment I concluded that I should be a teacher when I grew up and that I would be kind to my pupils. But I didn't know what subject.

"Then, a new teacher appeared in our fifth grade. She was young and pretty and just out of college and she spoke a tongue that no one understood. It was like music. It was English! And that was when I decided to become an English teacher."

Valentina takes the children through their English language paces, in circle games that involve every student in the room:

"I am twelve years old. How old are you?"

"I am eleven years old. How old are you?"

"Have you been to Moscow?"

"Yes, I have been to Moscow and the Caucasus. Where have you been?"

"I have been to the Urals. Where have you been?"

"What is your hobby?"

"My hobby is drawing. What is your hobby?"

"My hobby is all kinds of sports. What is your hobby?"

"My hobby is collecting stamps. What is your hobby?"

"My hobby is reading all kinds of books. What is your hobby?"

And on it goes in clear, articulate English with barely an accent.

Then the children perform two plays for me—*Robin Hood* and *Little Red Riding Hood*—complete with handmade costumes, hand-painted sets, and a genuine understanding of the lines the young actors delivered: "Once upon a time, there was a little girl who had a new pair of red shoes. She also had a grandmother who was very fond of her." I note that both texts are Walt Disney versions of the classic tales. Ah, American iconography.

Higher up in the Russian educational system English blooms. Katya Zarabova, a seventeen-year-old senior at School 105, is often our guide around Saint Petersburg. Each day she plies us with questions about the English language from a list she compiles from her reading: "Why do you say, 'Hi, there' when the person is nearby? Shouldn't it be 'Hi, here'?" "What is the origin of *OK*?" "Why do you call them blue-chip stocks?" "What is a jeep, and how did it get its name?" "What does 'total happening' mean?" "What's the difference between *convince* and *persuade*?"

Katya explains, "I began to study English because my older brother listened to American music, and I wanted to understand the words. Russian has a hard sound to it, but I like English because it is very soft. Speaking English is like chewing gum.

"A lot of English words you can already recognize in Russian—*OK, computer, toaster, mixer, coffee, Coca-Cola,* and *businessman.* And English is all through our sports—*football, dribble, basketball, baseball, volleyball, interview, derby,* and *champion.* Most of the kids like to use English words in their speech, especially slang works like *wow, oops, cool, awesome,* and *yeah* for *yes.* The more you use, the more popular you are."

Included in Tatyana Vereshkina cache of pupil compositions is a story by Irene Kosmina, a ten-year-old third grader, about a drawing room, with a "big, bright carpet," under which live an imaginary horse and tiger:

The animals are afraid of the volcano in the corner of the room. It has a special kind of power. Sometimes it has eruptions. The animals can hear loud sounds of music, cries of people, and some other things. They know that people call that volcano a TV set. The horse and the tiger are happy that they have Sheila as a friend. She is a real friend, not imaginary.

I wonder what has happened now that American television has erupted in Russian homes. I wonder what has happened now that small-screen technologies have invaded the nation. Do children still speak and write and act in English with such engaging maturity? Do three to five thousand people still come to the National Library reading room each day? Do row upon row of riders still sit in the metro reading books? I wonder what has happened to the astonishing verbalness of Russian culture.

THE
COLLIDE-O-SCOPE
OF LANGUAGE

How Wise Is Proverbial Wisdom?

A proverb is a well-known, venerable saying rooted in philosophical or religious wisdom. Just about everybody knows some proverbs, and we often base decisions on these instructive maxims. But when you line up proverbs that spout conflicting advice, you have to wonder if these beloved aphorisms aren't simply personal observations masquerading as universal truths:

- How can it be true that you should look before you leap, but make hay while the sun shines? It's better to be safe than sorry; but nothing ventured, nothing gained. Haste makes waste, but he who hesitates is lost. Patience is a virtue, but opportunity knocks but once. Slow and steady wins the race, but gather ye rosebuds while ye may. Fools rush in where angels fear to tread, but faint heart never won fair maiden. A stitch in time saves nine, but better late than never. Don't count your chickens before they're hatched, but forewarned is forearmed. Never put off till tomorrow what you can do today, but don't cross that bridge until you come to it. There's no time like the present, but well begun is half done. All things come to him who waits; but time and tide wait for no man, seize the day, and strike while the iron is hot.

- We often proclaim that actions speak louder than words, but at the same time we contend that the pen is mightier than the sword.

- Beware of Greeks bearing gifts, but don't look a gift horse in the mouth.

- There's no place like home, home is where the heart is, and don't burn your bridges behind you; but the grass is always greener on the other side, and a rolling stone gathers no moss.

- A penny saved is a penny earned, but penny wise and pound foolish.
- The best things in life are free, but you get what you pay for.
- A bird in the hand is worth two in the bush; but a man's reach should exceed his grasp, or what's a heaven for?
- Where ignorance is bliss, 'tis folly to be wise because what you don't know can't hurt you; but it is better to light one candle than to curse the darkness because the unexamined life is not worth living.
- Too many cooks spoil the broth, and two's company, but three's a crowd. On the other hand, many hands make light work, and two heads are better than one because the more the merrier.
- If at first you don't succeed, try, try again; but don't beat a dead horse.
- Fortune favors the brave, but discretion is the better part of valor.
- Silence is golden, talk is cheap, and actions speak louder than words; but the squeaky wheel gets the grease, and a word to the wise is sufficient.
- Clothes make the man because seeing is believing; but beauty is only skin deep because appearances are deceiving, you can't judge a book by its cover, still waters run deep, and all that glitters is not gold.
- Honesty is the best policy, but flattery will get you everywhere.
- All work and no play makes Jack a dull boy; but idle hands are the devil's workshop; and early to bed, early to rise makes a man healthy, wealthy, and wise.
- Birds of a feather flock together, but opposites attract. Blood is thicker than water, but familiarity breeds contempt.
- Boys will be boys; but spare the rod and spoil the child, and children should be seen but not heard.
- The road to hell is paved with good intentions, but it's the thoughts that counts.
- Ask me no questions, I'll tell you no lies; but ask and you shall receive, and knock, and it shall be opened unto you.

- Here today, gone tomorrow, but a thing of beauty is a joy forever. There is nothing permanent except change, and you never step in the same river twice; but there is nothing new under the sun and the more things change, the more they stay the same.

- You can't teach an old dog new tricks, and there's no fool like an old fool; but live and learn. Out of the mouths of babes comes wisdom; but older is wiser, and the older the violin the sweeter the music.

- Don't change horses in midstream; but a new broom sweeps clean, and variety is the spice of life.

- The bigger, the better, but the best things come in small packages.

- Absence makes the heart grow fonder, but out of sight, out of mind.

- What will be will be, but life is what you make it.

- When it rains, it pours; but lightning never strikes twice in the same place.

- Don't bite off more than you can chew, but hitch your wagon to a star.

- A miss is a good as a mile, but half a loaf is better than none.

- What's sauce for the goose is sauce for the gander, but one man's meat is another man's poison.

- Might makes right, and only the strong survive; but a soft answer turns away wrath, and the meek shall inherit the earth.

- Turn the other cheek, let bygones be bygones, and forgive and forget; but an eye for an eye and a tooth for a tooth because revenge is sweet, and turnabout is fair play.

- It's not whether you win or lose but how you play the game, and winning isn't everything; but to the victor goes the spoils.

- Share and share alike, but possession is nine-tenths of the law.

- Faith will move mountains; but if the mountain won't come to Mohammad, Mohammad must go to the mountain.

- Do unto others as you would have them do unto you, but all's fair in love and war.

- Virtue is its own reward; but no good deed goes unpunished, and only the good die young.

- Two wrongs don't make a right, but the ends justify the means.

So for better days ahead, all you have to do is figure out which proverb to use under which circumstances! Quite apparently, whichever side of an argument one takes, one can usually find a proverb to support it. That's why Miguel Cervantes wrote, "There is no proverb that is not true," while Lady Montagu proclaimed that "general notions are generally wrong."

Words That
Never Stray

What do the following words have in common: *beans*, *bread*, *chicken feed*, *clams*, *dough*, *cabbage*, *gravy*, *kale*, *lettuce*, *peanuts*, *spinach*, and *sugar*? Each is a food that is metaphoric slang for "cash."

What do these words have in common: *galore*, *extraordinaire*, *akimbo*, *aplenty*, *aweigh*, *incarnate*, *fatale*, *royale*, *par excellence*, *immemorial*, *aforethought*, and *manque*? The answer is that the dozen are "deferential words." While the vast majority of adjectives precede the nouns they modify, the words in this list always come after the nouns they modify.

What characteristic do the following words share: *any*, *arty*, *beady*, *cagey*, *cutie*, *decay*, *easy*, *empty*, *envy*, *essay*, *excel*, *excess*, *icy*, *ivy*, *kewpie*, *seedy*, and *teepee*? Turns out that each word is cobbled from the sounds of two letters—*NE, RT, BD, KG, QT, DK, EZ, MT, NV, SA, XL, XS, IC, IV, QP, CD,* and *TP*.

None of these clusters approaches the fascination of another group of words that I have been tracking for decades. Read on, O fellow verbivore, and I trust that the category will gradually come into focus.

Hoping to make some clean lucre to slake my hunger, I'm going to get a discussion in edgewise about a special category of words. Unless I give this topic long shrift, I'll be in rotten fettle. Please don't hurl aspersions at these words. I'd prefer that your dander and hackles be down and that you wait on tenterhooks with bated curiosity. Even after searching every cranny, don't just sit there gnashing your lips and twiddling your toes.

The above paragraph was pretty weird, wasn't it? In fact, it was anything but in kilter. That's because lucre can never be clean, only filthy, thirst is the only need that can be slaked, and only a word can be gotten in edgewise. Although some people are given a lot of time to shrive (confess), we can speak about shrift only as being short. Fettle must be fine, and aspersions can only be cast—never hurled, spoken, or written. Dander can be only gotten up and hackles raised. Nothing can ever be *off* tenterhooks, and *bated* can modify only *breath*. Crannies come only with nooks, and the only body parts we can gnash are our teeth and that we can twiddle are our thumbs.

What's so odd about words such as *lucre, slake, edgewise, shrift, fettle, aspersions, dander, hackles, tenterhooks, bated, cranny,* and *twiddle?* Their commonality is that they are always yoked to one— and only one—other word or phrase.

My kindred spirit (there's another one!) Al Gregory is a retired New York postman who lets neither snow, nor rain, nor heat, nor gloom of night stay him from delivering a clever idea in language. Al calls these "monogamous words" because they are always married to one specific word or phrase, and those marriages have withstood the ravages of time. Please bear in mind that a monogamous word is pledged to one—and only one—other word. Thus, an exhibit such as *daylights* doesn't quite qualify because it has two mates: *scare* and *beat*, as in "scare the daylights out of" and "beat the daylights out of." Similarly, *boggles* seems to me to be twice married—to *the mind* and *the imagination*—one can *wreak* havoc or vengeance, one can be taken or caught *unawares*, and *pickings* can be both *slim* or *easy*.

I also exclude reduplications, such as *razzle* dazzle, super *duper*, *namby pamby,* and *hurly burly,* and specialized medical terms, such as *anaphylactic* shock, sleep *apnea, carotid* artery, *circadian* rhythm, *ectopic* pregnancy, *macular* degeneration, and *varicose* veins.

Linguist and lexicographer David Grambs labels these idiosyncratic words "special-team players, not all-round or all-game players." Marshaling another analogy, Grambs writes, "Such words are today virtually one-idiom-only words, having almost no life in the English language beyond the discrete phrase they've become a part of, like fossilized insects preserved in amber."

Many of these single-idiom words have fascinating origins: *Shrift* is the noun form of *shrive,* "to confess before a priest." The compound *short shrift* originally referred to the brief time that a condemned prisoner had to make a confession and receive absolution. *Tenterhooks* are hooks that hold cloth on a tenter, a framework for stretching cloth. To be *on tenterhooks* is to be in a state of great tension or suspense. *Bated* is a shortened form of *abated.* That's why *waiting with bated breath* means waiting with breath held back.

Let's make a game of it. Here, alphabetically, are 130 additional examples of monogamous, special-team words. Fill in each blank with the one and only word or phrase that completes each idiom. Only after you've tried your very best may you turn to "Answers to Games and Quizzes."

1. _____ aback 2. _____ afield 3. _____ aforethought 4._____ aggrandizing 5. _____ akimbo 6. _____ amok 7. _____ arrears 8. artesian _____ 9. _____ askance 10. _____ astray

11. _____ _____ auspices _____ 12. _____ aweigh 13. _____ awry 14. bald-faced/barefaced _____ 15. _____ _____ behest 16. _____ bended _____ 17. bide _____ _____ 18. blithering _____ 19. bogged _____ 20. _____ _____ breather

21. breakneck _____ 22. briny _____ 23. _____ bumpkin 24. busman's _____ 25. _____ bygones _____ bygones 26._____ cahoots 27. champing _____ _____ _____ 28. dandle _____ _____ _____ 29. _____ dint _____ 30. dipsy _____

31. _____ drag-out 32. _____ _____ _____ _____druthers 33. _____ dudgeon 34. eke _____ 35.extenuating _____ 36. figment _____ _____ _____ 37. fine-tooth _____ 38. foregone _____ 39. _____ forfend 40. _____ _____ fritz

41. gainful _____ 42. _____ geezer 43. gibbous _____ 44. gird _____ _____ 45. grist _____ _____ _____ 46. gung _____ 47. _____ gussied _____ 48. halcyon _____ 49. _____ haywire 50. _____ heeler

51. hunker _____ 52. _____ immemorial 53. _____ inroads 54. _____ intentioned 55. _____ _____ kibosh _____ 56. _____ klatch 57. _____ _____ lam 58. lickety _____ 59. _____ lieu _____ 60. _____ loggerheads

61. _____ madding _____ 62. _____ _____ middling 63. misspent _____ 64. _____ muckamuck 65. neap _____ 66. noised _____
67._____ _____ nothings 68. _____ _____ nth _____ 69. _____ _____
offing 70. opposable _____

71. _____ _____ _____ petard 72. peter _____ 73. pinking _____
74. Pyrrhic _____ 75. raring _____ _____ 76. _____ riddance 77. _____
roughshod 78. rumpus _____ 79. runcible _____ 80. _____ sanctum

81. scot- _____ 82. _____ scruff _____ _____ _____ 83. self-fulfilling
_____ 84. _____ _____ shebang 85. shored _____ 86. sleight _____
_____ 87. suborn _____ 88. _____ suasion 89._____ _____ tat 90. _____
_____ thataway

91. _____ _____ throes _____ 92. toed _____ _____ 93. _____ _____
tizzy 94. _____ _____ trice 95. _____ trove 96. _____ turpitude 97.
ulterior _____ 98. _____ umbrage 99. unsung _____ 100. vale _____
_____

101. vantage _____ 102. wend _____ _____ 103. whiled _____ _____
_____ 104. _____ whippersnapper 105. wishful _____ 106. _____ _____
_____ _____ wont 107. workaday _____ 108. _____ wroth 109. _____
_____ yore 110. zoot _____

Now try some pairs connected by *and*:
111. _____ and abet 112. _____ and alack 113. _____ be-all and
_____ 114. beck and _____ 115. betwixt and _____ 116. _____ and caboodle 117. dribs and _____ 118. _____ and fro 119. hale and _____
120. _____ and haw

121. _____ _____ intents and _____ 122. kith and _____ 123. null
and _____ 124. pomp and _____ 125. spick and _____ 126. _____ and
thither 127. _____ and tribulations 128. vim and _____ 129. whys and
_____ 130. _____ and yon

Heads Without Tails

When a pig gets laryngitis, is it then disgruntled? But seriously . . .

What do you make of the fact that we can talk about certain things and ideas only when they are absent? Once they appear, our confounding English language doesn't allow us to describe them. Have you ever run into someone who was gruntled, combobulated, sheveled, chalant, plussed, ruly, gainly, maculate, kempt, pecunious, peccable, or souciant?

English is a language populated by a lot of heads without tails and odds without ends. These words and expressions are like single socks nestled in a drawer: they never become part of a pair.

Have you ever seen a horseful carriage or a strapful gown? Have you ever met a sung hero or experienced requited love? I know people who are no spring chickens, but where, pray tell, are the people who *are* spring chickens? Where are the people who actually *would* hurt a fly? All the time I meet people who *are* great shakes, who actually *did* squat, who *can* cut the mustard, who *can* fight City Hall, who *are* my cup of tea, who *would* lift a finger to help, who *do* have a mean bone in their body, who *would* give you the time of day, and whom I *would* touch with a ten-foot pole, but I can't talk about them in English—and that *is* a laughing matter.

These negatives that lack corresponding positives have been labeled "unnegatives," and they are close kin to "unplurals"—plurals that are not made from singulars. Like *gruntled, sheveled,* and *combobulated,* we behold another category of heads without tails.

Doesn't it seem just a little wifty that we can make amends but never just one amend and that no matter how carefully we comb through the annals of history, we can never explore just one annal?

Why can't a moderately messy room be in a shamble? Why can't a moderately indebted person be in an arrear? Why can't moderately conspiratorial people be in a cahoot?

Why is it that we can never pull a shenanigan, consume an egg Benedict, be in a doldrum, or experience just one jitter, willy, delirium tremen, or heebie-jeebie? Why, sifting through the wreckage of a room blown to smithereens, can we never find just one smithereen?

Indeed, this whole business of plurals that don't have matching singulars reminds me to ask this burning question, one that has flummoxed scholars for centuries: If you have a bunch of odds and ends and you get rid of or sell off all but one of them, what do you call that single item you're left with?

Our Uppity Language

It's time to catch up on *up*, the ever-present two-letter word that may have more meanings than any other and, at times, no meaning at all. It's easy to understand *up* when it means skyward or toward the top of a list. And clearly there are crucial differences between *call* and *call up* and *beat* and *beat up*. But I have to wonder why we warm ourselves up, why we speak up, why we shower up, why a topic comes up, and why we crack up at a joke.

Let's face up to it: We're all mixed up about *up*. Usually the little word is totally unnecessary. Why do we light up a cigar, lock up the house, polish up the silverware, and fix up the car when we can more easily and concisely light, lock, polish, and fix them?

At times, verbs with *up* attached mess up our heads and mess up our minds with bewildering versatility. To look up a chimney means one thing, to look up a friend another, to look up to a mentor yet another, to look up a word something else. We can make up a bed, a story, a test, our face, and our mind, and each usage has a completely different meaning.

At other times, *up-* verbs are unabashedly ambiguous. When we wind up our watch, we start it; when we wind up a meeting, we stop it. When we hold up our partners on the tennis court, are we supporting or hindering them? How, pray tell, can we walk up and down the aisle at the same time and slow up and slow down at the same time?

What bollixes up our language worse than anything else is that *up* can be downright misleading. A house doesn't really burn up; it burns down. We don't really throw up; we throw out and down. We don't pull up a chair; we pull it along. Most of us don't add up a column of figures; we add them down.

And why is it that we first chop down a tree, and then we chop it up?

Maybe it's time to give up on the uppity *up*.

On Palindromes

The ancient and popular Art of the Palindrome blazes out from the epicenter of the universe of letter play. Alistair Reid expresses what may be the very heart of the fascination for matters palindromic when he writes, "The dream which occupies the tortuous mind of every palindromist is that somewhere within the confines of the language lurks the Great Palindrome, the nutshell which not only fulfills the intricate demands of the art, flowing sweetly in both directions, but which also contains the Final Truth of Things." There is indeed something magic about the palindromic craft, the platonic form of making the alphabet dance.

In March, 1926, the San Diego Zoological Society published the first volume of its magazine and came up with the title *ZOONOOZ*, a palindrome that works both rightside up and upside down. While the eighty-year-old *ZOONOOZ* is an outstanding example of the palindromic art and craft, the most elegant palindromic statements have been born during the last forty years, since the publication of Dmitri Borgmann's *Language on Vacation* and the birth of *Word Ways*.

In the quirkily brilliant *I Love Me, Vol. I*, Michael Donner explains perspicaciously that palindromania has "at last [been] correctly understood to be not a disorder at all but rather the heightened sense of order we now know it to be." To help bring order to the universe of palindromes, I offer some rubrics for creating, identifying, and ranking great palindromes.

The brevity and simplicity of single-word palindromes, such as LEVEL, REDDER, and ROTATOR, make them relatively less surprising and elegant than longer and more challenging palindromic statements. Word-unit palindromes, such as FAIR IS FOUL, AND FOUL IS FAIR; FIRST LADIES RULE THE STATE, AND STATE THE RULE—"LADIES

FIRST!"; and YOU CAN CAGE A SWALLOW CAN'T YOU, BUT YOU CAN'T SWALLOW A CAGE, CAN YOU? are only a half step above. Donner observes, "Composing word-unit palindromes is an entirely different kettle of fish from composing letter-unit palindromes. . . . The word-unit composer seems to require as good a grasp of syntactic possibilities as the letter-unit composer requires of spelling possibilities. The only catch is that the two types of familiarity are quite distinct and perhaps equally hard to acquire."

Reverse whole-word reversal palindromes, such as STEP ON NO PETS, RATS LIVE ON NO EVIL STAR, and the widely circulated ABLE WAS I ERE I SAW ELBA also lack surprise. I agree with Borgmann when he says that such constructions are "really a sign of inferior craftsmanship, since almost anyone can juggle palindromic words and reversals around in almost mechanical fashion until a meaningful group of words emerges. . . . [W]hat requires genuine skill is the construction of a palindromic sentence which, read in reverse, has each word sliding over from one to another into the words used in the frontward reading." The reconfiguring in the second half of the letter clusters and separating spaces in the first half of a palindromic statement contributes surprise and elegance to the adventure in letter play.

Prize palindromic statements also exhibit subject-verb structure. Cobbling a subject-verb palindromic statement is harder to pull off and, hence, more elegant when the result is successful. Moreover, subject-verb syntax inspires the reader to conjure up a clearer image of persons or things in action. IF I HAD A HI-FI; LID OFF A DAFFODIL; and even the famous A MAN! A PLAN! A CANAL! PANAMA! do not amaze the readers and conjure visions that dance in their heads as delightfully as do NURSE, I SPY GYPSIES. RUN!, SIT ON A POTATO PAN, OTIS, and STOP! MURDER US NOT, TONSURED RUMPOTS!

This matter of imagery is crucial to the greatness of a palindrome. The highest-drawer palindromic statements invoke a picture of the world that is a bubble off plumb yet somehow of our world. One *could* warn one's nurse that gypsies are nearby. Someone named Otis *could* sit on a potato pan, and shorn drunkards *could* seek to do us grave bodily harm.

Two of my favorite subject-verb palindromes are the ELK CITY, KANSAS, IS A SNAKY TICKLE and DOC, NOTE. I DISSENT. A FAST NEVER PREVENTS A FATNESS. I DIET ON COD. But as delightfully loopy as the first specimen is and as astonishing in its length and coherence as the second three-sentence jawdropper is, they do not summon vivid images to cavort in our mind's eye.

Using the rubrics of

- elegance,
- surprise,
- reconfiguration of the letter clusters and spaces in the first half,
- subject-verb structure,
- bizarre imagery,

I submit that the greatest palindrome ever cobbled is GO HANG A SALAMI. I'M A LASAGNA HOG.

The Long and the Short of English

We humans are fascinated with the largest and smallest of all manner of things—giants and dwarfs, the most colossal and miniature animals, the tallest and lowest buildings and trees. Wordaholics! Logolepts! Verbivores of all ages! Step right up to an exhibit of some of the most fascinating specimens of all—the longest and shortest words!

- **Longest word in standard English dictionaries:** *pneumonoultramicroscopicsilicovolcanoconiosis,* a forty-five-letter term for black lung disease contracted by miners.

- **Longest words in common use:** *counterrevolutionaries* and *deinstitutionalization,* both twenty-two letters.

- **Longest one-syllable word:** *squirreled.*

- **Longest word with a single vowel:** *strengths.*

- **Longest isogram,** a word in which no letter is repeated: *uncopyrightable.*

- **Longest grammagrams,** words consisting entirely of letter sounds: *expediency,* which can be represented as *XPDNC; effeminacy (FMNSE),* and *obediency (OBDNC).*

- **Longest homophonic anagram,** that is, two words that are spelled differently but that sound alike and that contain the same letters: *discrete - discreet.*

- **Longest heteronyms,** two words that are spelled the same but are pronounced differently: *unionized* (the presence of labor unions) and *unionized* (not ionized).

- **Longest capitonym,** a capitalized word that changes pronunciation when lowercased: *Breathed* (*Opus* cartoonist Berkeley Breathed) and *breathed.*

- **Longest anagrammable words:** *conversationalists - conservationalists.*

- **Longest common palindromic word,** one that can be read backward and forward: *redivider.*

- **Longest uncommon palindromic word:** *kinnikkinnik,* a mixture of sumac leaves, dogwood bark, and bearberry smoked by the Cree Nation in the Ohio Valley.

- **Longest palindromic word in another language:** *saippuakivikauppias,* a nineteen-letter Finnish word designating a soap or lye dealer.

- **Longest words that are reverse images of each other:** *stressed - desserts.* How fortuitous! When you feel stressed, eat desserts.

- **Longest words with switchable halves:** *barstool - toolbars, mentally - tallymen,* each eight letters.

- **Longest univocalic word,** one that contains a single vowel repeated: *strengthlessness.*

- **Longest snowball word,** composed of words that increase one letter at a time: *temperamentally,* which can be divided into *t em per amen tally.*

- **Longest reverse snowball word:** *plainclothesmen,* which can be divided into *plain clot he's me n.*

- **Longest kangaroo word:** Inside *rambunctious* appear, in order, the letters in the smaller synonym *raucous.*

- **Longest words with letters in alphabetical order:** *Aegilops,* meaning "an ulcer in part of the eye," is an eight-letter word in which all letters proceed in alphabetical order with no double letters. But let's admit that *aegilops* is pretty obscure. Using more common words, we can get up to six letters: *abhors, almost, begins, bijoux, biopsy, chimps, chinos,* and *chintz.*

- **Longest word with the most letters in alphabetical place:** In *archetypical,* the letters *a, c, e, i,* and *l* each appear in their natural slots in the alphabet.

- **Longest word that can be beheaded:** Remove the first letter of *presidentially* and you are left with *residentially.*

- **Longest word that can be curtailed:** Remove the last letter of the word *bulleting* and you are left with *bulletin*.
- **Longest words that can integrate all five major vowels:** *blander - blender - blinder - blonder - blunder; patting - petting - pitting - potting - putting.*
- **Longest word lacking a major vowel:** *rhythms.*
- **Longest words that can be typed on a single horizontal row of a typewriter:** The ten-letter words *pepperroot, peppertree, pepperwort, perpetuity, proprietor, repertoire,* and—ta da!—*typewriter* can all be typed on the qwerty row.
- **Shortest word with all five major vowels:** *sequoia.*
- **Shortest famous name with all five major vowels:** (Grace) Metalious, author of *Peyton Place.*
- **Shortest common word with *aeiou* in order:** *facetious.*
- **Shortest uncommon word with *aeiou* in order:** *aresious.*
- **Shortest word with *aeiou* in reverse order:** *unnoticeably.*
- **Shortest word without a vowel:** *nth.*
- **Shortest word in which one letter appears five times:** *assesses.*
- **Shortest heteronym,** a word pronounced two different ways with two different meanings: *do.*
- **Shortest capitonyms,** words that change sound and meaning when lowercased: *Guy* and *Job.*
- **Shortest readable pangrams,** statements that use the twenty-six letters of the alphabet: *Mr. Jock, TV quiz Ph.D., bags few lynx* and *The glib czar junks my VW Fox PDQ.* Both these pangrams contain only twenty-six letters.
- **Shortest verse in the Bible:** "Jesus wept" (John 11:35).
- **Shortest poems:**

On the Antiquity of Microbes
Adam
Had 'em.

On the Questionable Importance of the Individual
I . . .
Why?

- **Shortest speech ever recorded:** The surrealist painter Salvador Dali said, "I will be so brief that I have already finished." And he sat down.

- **Shortest correspondence:** In 1862, the French author Victor Hugo was on holiday. Eager to know how his new novel, *Les Miserables,* was selling, Hugo wrote his New York publisher: "?" Came the reply: "!"

- **Shortest sentence** (only three letters): "I am."

- **Longest sentence** (pun alert!): "I do."

THE ROMANCE
OF WORDS

Toothsome
Etymologies

To the man or woman who knows its origin, each word presents a picture, no matter how ordinary it may appear. Sometimes the attrition wrought by time and human memory has ravaged the images so that no trace is left. In other instances surface grime can be wiped away so that the beauty of the details can be restored and the contours and colors can once again be seen.

For me word pictures are like family snapshots. Discovering the origin of a word or phrase gives me the same pleasure I used to experience when my grandparents, parents, and older brothers and sisters would open up the family album, point to a cluster of sepia photographs, and tell me stories about the people gazing out from the pages. Hearing tales about those who came before me and uncovering those odd, buried, Old World family mysteries helped me to learn whence I came and who I am.

Words too are our forebears. Most were born long before we were, and all bequeath us their rich legacies. Illuminating the faded picture of a time-hallowed word or phrase throws light on our history and our customs, our loving and fighting, our working and playing, our praying and our cursing.

The poet William Cowper once wrote of

philologists who trace
A panting syllable through time and space,
Start it at home, and hunt it in the dark
To Gaul, to Greece, and into Noah's ark.

As an avid word hunter-gatherer, I love stalking bestial words through time and flushing out the animals that live in the ark of language. Cranberries acquired their name from the Low German *kranbeere,* meaning "crane," because the plant flourishes in marshy lands frequented by cranes. Tiny mice scamper through our bodies because *muscle* derives metaphorically from the Latin *musculus,* diminutive of *mus,* "mouse." A scapegoat was an actual goat upon whose head were symbolically placed all the sins of the ancient Hebrew community. As we read in the book of Leviticus, the animal was allowed to "escape" into the wilderness, bearing the community's burden of sin and atoning for its transgressions.

If a scapegoat was really a goat, one might wonder, does a dandelion have anything to do with lions? Most certainly. The English used to call the yellow, shaggy weed a "lion's tooth" because the indented ("made jagged, as with a tooth"), pointed leaves resemble the lion's snarly grin. During the early fourteenth century the lion's-tooth plant took on a French flavor and became the *dent-de-lion,* "tooth-of-the-lion." Then it acquired an English accent: *dandelion.*

Toothsome etymologies such as the one for *dandelion* are of great assistance when I am invited to address various dental societies. A number of dentists will tell you that getting me to sit still in a dentist's chair is like pulling teeth. As a born coward, I am simply unable to transcend dental medication. Still, I was delighted to find out that the oral metaphors in our language provided a topic that I could really sink my teeth into.

At first I thought that expressions about the teeth would be as scarce as hen's teeth. (Hens, of course, don't have any teeth.) As I began collecting ideas for my talk to the dental societies, I believed that I would give my eyeteeth for some good examples.

The eyeteeth, I discovered, are so called because they are located directly below the eyes in the upper jaw and are called canine teeth because they resemble the pointed teeth of dogs. As such, they are especially useful in holding and tearing food, and they are the most difficult and painful of teeth to extract. Thus, if you would give your eyeteeth for something, you are willing to go through a lot to relinquish something of great value.

Teeth are often cited to indicate strength. We talk about an agreement that has teeth in it and being in the teeth of a battle fighting tooth and nail. We describe strong winds and sarcastic comments as "biting."

Not surprisingly, teeth are also associated with matters culinary. We call some women toothsome, not because they have a lot of teeth, but because their appearance is pleasing to the palate of the eyes. In parts of the country, Italian sandwiches are called grinders because it takes a good set of teeth to eat them. Pasta should be cooked *al dente,* "to the tooth"—in other words, cooked just enough to retain a somewhat firm texture for the teeth. Spanish cookbooks call for using a *diente* from a *cabeza* of garlic—that is, a "tooth" from a "head" of garlic.

Teeth are often associated with duplicity. We talk about people who *lie through their teeth,* that is, who force themselves to assume a calm demeanor that will conceal their true feelings. They display a hearty smile, baring and clenching their teeth as a means of controlling their emotions and pretending that *butter wouldn't melt in their mouths.* Closely related is the expression *to laugh on the wrong side of one's mouth,* which originally meant to laugh in a forced way, perhaps by opening only one corner of the mouth. "Which side of the mouth is the wrong side?" we wonder aloud.

Many phrases from the Book of Job in the Old Testament have become proverbial in our language: "Naked came I from my mother's womb, and naked shall I return"; "The Lord gave, and the Lord hath taken away"; and "My bone cleaveth to my skin, and to my flesh, and I am escaped with the skin of my teeth." This last phrase has been altered slightly to *by the skin of my teeth.*

Despite objections that the teeth don't have any skin, centuries of Bible reading have given the expression a permanent place in our language as a description of a close escape. Many interpret the skin in *skin of my teeth* to refer to the enamel covering the teeth, a film as thin as Job's margin of safety.

As with *dandelion,* animals and teeth converge in *mastodon,* the name we assign to those lumbering pre-elephants. *Mastodon* is cobbled from the Greek *mastos,* "breast," (as in *mastectomy*) and *odont,* "tooth," as in *orthodontia* ("correct teeth"). Mastodons are so named for the nipplelike protuberances on their molars. Rats, mice, squirrels, chipmunks, and beavers get their Latin name from their teeth.

Given these creatures' proclivity to chew, chew, chew, it's no surprise that they get their family name from the verb "to gnaw."

The space I've left at the start of each paragraph in this book is an *indentation.* When we indent a paragraph (from the Latin *dens,* "tooth," by way of the French *dent*), we take a chunk, or small bite, out of the beginning. *Indenture,* from the same root, strictly means "a document with serrated edges," referring to the once-common practice of cutting contracts into halves with jagged edges—one half for each party. By fitting the edges together, one could authenticate the document.

When we describe a golden ager as *long in the tooth,* we are reflecting the fact that our gums recede with age, thereby displaying more and more roots. It's the same with horses. The age and health of a horse can be ascertained by examining the condition and number of its teeth. Although an animal may appear young and frisky, a close inspection may reveal that it is *long in the tooth* and ready for the glue factory.

Still, it is considered bad manners to inspect the teeth of a horse that has been given to you and, by extension, to inquire too closely into the cost or value of any gift. Now you know the origin of *don't look a gift horse in the mouth,* one of our oldest proverbs, whinnying back at least fifteen hundred years.

If, on the other hoof, you decide to pay money to a horse trader, you are advised to determine whether it is a young stud or an old nag by examining the teeth and obtaining your information *straight from the horse's mouth,* precisely where responsible word-searchers should look.

Haunted Words

The Greek *etymon* means "true, original," and the Greek ending *-logia* means "science or study." Thus, etymology is supposed to be the science or study of true and original word meanings. But I have learned that the proud house of etymology is populated by all manner of ghoulies and ghosties and long-leggety beasties miscreated by spook etymologists. (*Spook* reaches back to the Dutch *spooc,* "ghost, specter.") These sham scholars would rather invent a word origin after the fact than trace it to its true source. Spooks prefer drama and romance to accuracy and truth. With spooks it is sentence first, trial never.

Caveat lexamator: Word lover beware. Be wary especially of explanations of labels for food. Eating humble pie has nothing etymologically to do with the word *humble,* "lowly." The dish was really *umble pie,* made from the umbles—heart, liver, and other innards—of a deer. The servants and huntsmen had to settle for these innards while the lord of the manor and his guests dined on venison. *Sirloin* is not so called because James I or Henry VIII (according to Thomas Fuller in 1655) or Charles II (according to *Cook's Oracle* in 1822) knighted his favorite dish, declaring, "Arise, Sir Loin." In truth, *sirloin,* the upper or choicer part of a loin of beef, was borrowed from Middle French *surloigne (sur,* "above" + *loigne,* "loin") centuries before any of the monarchs who are credited with honoring the cut of meat. But legends die hard, especially when they are lit by such bright stories, and this particular flight of etymological fancy has survived for more than three centuries as a hoax of wordplay foisted on unsuspecting language lovers.

More culinary spookery has been served up in the game of tennis, where *love* means "no points." The most charming derivation for the use of *love* in this sense is that the word derives from *l'ouef* —"the egg"—because a zero resembles an egg, just as the Americanism "goose egg" stands for "zero." But *un oeuf,* rather than *l'ouef,* would be the more likely French form, and, anyway, the French themselves (and most other Europeans) designate "no score" in tennis by saying "zero." Most tennis historians adhere to a less imaginative but more plausible theory. These more level heads contend that the tennis term is rooted in the Old English expression "neither love nor money," which is more than a thousand years old. Because love is the antithesis of money, it is nothing.

One of the most persistent and spookiest of etymologies is the recurrent wheeze that *posh,* "elegant, swanky," is an acronym for "p(ort) o(ut), s(tarboard) h(ome)," a beguiling bit of linguistic legerdemain that has taken in a company of estimable scholars. When British colonial emissaries and wealthy vacationers made passage to and from India and the Orient, they often traveled along the coast of Africa on the Peninsular and Oriental Steam Navigation Company line. Many of these travelers sought ideal accommodations "away from the weather," on the more comfortable or shady side of the ship. By paying for two staterooms—one portside out, the other starboard home—the very rich could avoid the blazing sun and strong winds both ways, an act of conspicuous consumption that has become synonymous with anything luxurious and ultrasmart.

While the abundant inventiveness here deserves at least a sitting ovation, this etymology of *posh* is, well, bosh. For one thing, neither the travelers' literature of the period nor the records of the famous Peninsular and Oriental Steam Navigation Company show a jot of reference to *posh.* For another, an examination of the deck plans of the ships of the period reveals that the cabins were not placed on the port and starboard sides. For a third, *posh* does not show up in print until 1918. For a fourth, always be suspicious of etymologies that employ acronyms: *cop* does not stand for "constable on patrol" nor *tip,* as a gratuity, for "to insure promptness" nor *news* for "northeast-west-south" nor *golf* for "gentlemen only; ladies forbidden" nor you-know-what for "for unlawful carnal knowledge."

The editors of the *Oxford English Dictionary* say nothing of any connection with the location of cabins on ships and either ignore or reject outright the acronymic theory, and all Merriam-Webster dictionaries list the origin as "unknown." Moreover, the monsoon winds that blow in and out of the Asian heartland shift from winter to summer. This fickle phenomenon changes the location of the sheltered and exposed sides of a ship so that in a given season the ideal location can be starboard out, portside home (hence, *soph*). More likely and more mundanely, *posh* hails from a British slang word of the same spelling that means "a dandy."

Spook etymologies are haunting your computer, in the form of a ubiquitous item titled "Life in the 1500s" that has been dragging its chains around the Internet for years. The color and romance of the word and phrase explanations in the message are as beguiling as can be. One of them is this electronic explanation of a common meteorological phrase: "Houses had thatched roofs. Thick straw, piled high, with no wood underneath. It was the only place for animals to get warm, so all the pets—dogs, cats, mice, rats, and bugs—lived in the roof. When it rained, it became slippery, and sometimes the animals would slip and fall off the roof. Hence the saying *It's raining cats and dogs*."

You'll also hear that in the Dark Ages, people believed that animals, including cats and dogs, had magical powers. Cats were associated with storms, especially the black cats of witches, while dogs were frequently associated with winds. The Norse storm god Odin was frequently shown surrounded by dogs and wolves. So when a particularly violent storm came along, people would say that *it's raining cats and dogs,* with the cats symbolizing the rain and the dogs representing the wind and storm.

But the truth appears to be more mundane. Cats and dogs make a lot of noise when they fight (hence, "fighting like cats and dogs"), so they have become a metaphor for a noisy rain or thunderstorm.

The "Internetymology" continues: "Sometimes they could obtain pork and would feel really special when that happened. When company came over, they would bring out some bacon and hang it to show it off. It was a sign of wealth and that a man could really bring *home the bacon*. They would cut off a little to share with guests and would all sit and *chew the fat.*"

Ridiculous. Absurd. Here the bacon refers to the greased pig that once figured so prominently in American county fairs. The slippery swine was awarded to whoever caught it, and the winner could take (bring) it home.

Chew the fat is unknown before the American Civil War. One theory contends that sailors working their jaws on the tough salt pork rationed out when supplies ran low constantly grumbled about their poor fare while literally chewing the fat. What seems clear is that chewing the fat, like shooting the breeze, provides little sustenance for the amount of mastication involved. Which is just what happens with jerry-built, jury-rigged etymologies.

Now the plot deepens, and our subject turns grave. Some of the most spookily haunted of the explanations in "Life in the 1500s" pertain to death: "Lead cups were used to drink ale or whiskey. The combination would sometimes knock people out for a couple of days. Someone walking along the road would take them for dead and prepare them for burial. They were laid out on the kitchen table for a couple of days and the family would gather around and eat and drink and wait and see if they would wake up. Hence the custom of holding a 'wake.'"

Folderol! Piffle! Poppycock! *Wake* descends from the Middle English *wakien,* "to be awake," and is cognate with the Latin *vigil. Wake* simply means that someone stays awake all night at the side of the casket on the night before the funeral.

Hear ye now the most ghoulish and foolish of the spook etymologies that clank throughout this e-dissertation: "England is old and small, and they started running out of places to bury people. So they would dig up coffins and would take their bones to a house and reuse the grave. In reopening these coffins, one out of twenty-five coffins were found to have scratch marks on the inside, and they realized they had been burying people alive. So they thought they would tie a string on their wrist and lead it through the coffin and up through the ground and tie it to a bell. Someone would have to sit out in the graveyard all night to listen for the bell. Hence the expression *grave-yard shift.* They would know that someone was *saved by the bell* or he was *a dead ringer."*

Balderdash! Twaddle! Hooey! Codswollop! Despite high marks for ingenuity, these etymological explanations are merely exercises in free association without regard for attribution. In factories that work around the clock, employees report for work at 8 a.m. for the "regular" or "day" shift; at 4 p.m. for the "swing" or "night" shift and at midnight for the "graveyard" shift, lasting until 8 a.m. According to Harold Wentworth and Stuart Berg Flexner's *Dictionary of American Slang,* the name *graveyard shift* refers to "the ghostlike hour of employment"—and nothing more.

Dead ringers actually originated at the race track. To take advantage of the long odds against an inferior horse's winning a race, unscrupulous gamblers would substitute a horse of superior ability and similar appearance. Nowadays, *dead ringer* means any close look-alike.

Why *ringer*? Probably because *ringer* was once a slang term for a counterfeiter who represented brass rings for gold ones at county fairs. And *dead* here means "absolute, exact," as in "dead heat" and "you're dead right."

Should I even dignify the windy suspiration about *saved by the bell* with a logical explanation? Oh well, here 'tis, and it's just what you thought in the first place. *Saved by the bell* is nothing more than the obvious—a reference to the bell signaling the end of a round of boxing. No matter what condition a fighter is in during a boxing contest, even if he is being counted out, he is saved by the bell and gains a reprieve once that bell rings.

I do hope that we all gain a reprieve from these idiotic spook etymologies that rattle and clank around the Internet and haunt the halls of our language. That, of course, is the same Internet that knowledgeably informs us that National Public Radio is about to go out of business; that Congress is about to institute an e-mail tax; that a virus is about to crash your computer; that your toilet is about to explode; that antiperspirants, Canola Oil, and NutraSweet cause just about every malady known to humankind; that Nieman Marcus charges $250 for a chocolate-chip cookie recipe; that a Nigerian businessman will make you rich if you will just make a modest deposit in his account; that 450 years ago Nostradamus predicted the outcome of the 2000 election, 9/11, and other history-changing events; and that next July we collide with Mars. If you believe everything you glean from cyberspace, especially about language, please get in touch with me. I have a bridge, a lovely parcel of swampland, and a subprime mortgage I want to sell you.

My Kids
the Poker Players

You're reading a book written by the most successful breeder of world-class poker professionals in history.

My son, Howard "The Professor" Lederer, and daughter, Annie Duke, live and move and have their beings in that windowless, clock-less pleasure dome known as Las Vegas. I'm pleased to report that they are the only sibling pair ever both to reach the final day of a World Series of Poker event and to have won national tournaments with capacious and impressive names, such as the Diamond Jim Brady Texas Hold'em Shootout, the Four Queens Poker Classic in No-Limit Omaha, and the Hall of Fame Classic Deuce-to-Seven Lowball Draw No-Limit. Whew.

My children's achievements in the gaming halls inspire me to deal from a full deck of vivid words and phrases that have made the trip from the poker table into our everyday conversation and writing. The color and high-risk excitement of poker have made the language of the game one of the most pervasive metaphors in our language.

The basic elements of poker are the cards, the chips, and the play of the hand, and each has become embedded in our daily parlance. Beginning with the cards themselves, the verb *to discard* descends from *decard*, "away card," and first meant to reject a card from one's hand. Gradually, the meaning of *discard* has broadened to include rejection beyond card-playing. A cardsharp who is out to cheat you may be dealing from the bottom of the deck and giving you a fast shuffle, in which case you may get lost in the shuffle. You might call such a low-down skunk a *four-flusher. Flush,* a hand of five cards that are all of one suit, flows from the Latin *fluxus* because all the cards flow together. *Four-flusher* characterizes a poker player who pretends to such good fortune but in fact holds a worthless hand of four same-suit cards and one that doesn't match.

All of these terms originated with poker and other betting card games and have undergone a process that linguists call broadening. A good example of movement from one specific argot to another is *wild card berth* or *wild card player* as used in football and tennis. In these sports, a team hopes for *back-to-back victories*—from a fortuitous ace-down-ace-up as the first two cards in a game of five-card stud.

Now that I've laid my cards on the table, let's see what happens when the chips are down. Why do we call a gilt-edged, sure-thing stock *a blue-chip stock?* Because poker chips are white, red, and blue, and the blue ones were traditionally the most valuable. Why, when we compare the value and power of two things, do we often ask how one *stacks up* against the other, as in "How do the Red Sox stack up against the Yankees?" Here the reference is to the columns of chips piled up before the players around a poker table. These stacks of plastic betting markers also account for the expressions *bottom dollar* and *top dollar*. *Betting one's bottom dollar* means wagering the entire stack, and the top dollar, or chip, is the one that sits atop the highest pile on the table. Indeed, the metaphor of poker chips is so powerful that one of the euphemisms we use for death is *cashing in one's chips*.

The guts of poker is the betting. *You bet!* has become a standard affirmative in American English, and it is far from being the only betting metaphor that has traveled from the gaming halls to our common vocabulary. If you want to call my bluff on that one and insist that I put up or shut up, I'll be happy to put my money where my mouth is.

Say you're involved in a big business deal. You let the other guy know that you're not a piker running a penny ante operation and that he'd better ante up big. One theory traces *piker,* one who habitually makes small bets, to westward migrants from Pike County, Missouri. These small farmers were less inclined than hardened veterans to risk high stakes, and the county name became eponymously synonymous with penny-pinching cheapness. *Ante,* from the Latin for "before," refers to chips placed in the middle of the poker table before the betting begins, so a penny ante game is fit only for pikers.

The negotiations continue, and you sweeten the pot by upping the stakes. You don't want to blow your wad and go in the hole or in hock, but you don't want to stand pat either. Rather than passing the buck, you play it close to the vest without showing your hand, maintain an inscrutable poker face, keep everything aboveboard, and hope to hit the jackpot.

The hole in the phrase *in the hole* refers to a slot cut in the middle of poker tables through which checks and cash are deposited into a box, to be transferred later to the coffers of the house. *In hock* descends from the game of faro, a cousin of poker. The last card in the box was known as the hocketty card. The player who bet that card was said to be *in hock,* at a disadvantage that could lose him his shirt.

Stand pat comes from the strategy of keeping one's original (pat) hand in draw poker rather than making an exchange. Because card-sharps are known to engage in chicanery when their hands are out of sight and under the table, or board, *aboveboard* has come to mean open honesty and *under the table* the opposite. *Playing it close to the vest* ensures that no one else will peek at the contents of a player's hand. *Jackpot* originally described the reward to the big winner in a game of progressive poker, in which you need a pair of jacks or better to "open the pot." Because the stakes grow higher until the requisite pair is dealt, *jackpot* has gradually expanded to include the pots of gold in slot machines, game shows, and state lotteries.

Pass the buck is a cliché that means "to shift responsibility." But why, you may have asked yourself, should handing someone a dollar bill indicate that responsibility is in any way transferred? Once again the answer can be found in high-stakes gaming halls and riverboats. The *buck* in *pass the buck* was originally a poker term designating a marker that was placed in front of the player whose turn it was to deal the next hand. This was done to vary the order of betting and to keep one person from dealing all the time, thus transferring the disadvantages of being the first to wager and cutting down on the chances of cheating. During the heyday of poker in the nineteenth century, the marker was often a hunting knife whose handle was made of a buck's horn. The marker defined the game as Buckhorn Poker or Buck Poker and gave us the expression *pass the buck.*

In the Old West, silver dollars often replaced buckhorn knives as tokens, and these coins took on the slang name *buck*. Former president Harry S. Truman, reputed to be a skillful poker player, adopted the now-famous motto "The buck stops here," meaning that the ultimate responsibility rested with the president.

The cleverest application of poker terminology that I have ever encountered appears on the truck of a New Hampshire plumbing company: "A Flush Is Better Than a Full House." In poker that isn't true, but a homeowner would recognize its wisdom.

Great poker players must have a firm grounding in the statistics of card distribution and probability. But, as my son and daughter the poker champions explain, "To play poker at the highest level is to read people—their faces, their body language, and their behavior patterns." Language and people are inextricably intertwined. The democratic poetry of poker that pervades our American language is a vivid emblem of the games that we, as a civilization, watch and play.

It's in the cards. You can bet on it.

On Paradox

In the last chapter, you learned that my son, Howard, and daughter, Annie, are professional poker players who have won millions of dollars at the gaming tables. It's an easy life—earning thousands of dollars in a single night just sitting around playing card games. But it's a hard-knock life, too, what with the long, sedentary hours; the addictive behavior and secondhand smoke that suffuse the poker rooms; and the times when Lady Luck goes out whoring and your pocketbook and ego get mugged.

How best to catch and crystallize this collide-o-scopic life my children lead, this life of gorgeous poker rooms and hearts of darkness, of Euclidean clarity and survival of the meanest? Bob "Silver Eagle" Thompson, once tournament director of the World Series of Poker at Binion's Horseshoe casino, said it best: "Poker is a tough way to make an easy living."

That's a paradox, a statement that seems absurd or self-contradictory but that turns out to be true. The word *paradox* combines *para*, "against," and *doxos*, "opinion, belief." In its Greek form the word meant "not what you'd expect to be true."

Paradox is a particularly powerful device to ensnare truth because it concisely tells us something that we did not know we knew. It engages our hearts and minds because, beyond its figurative employment, paradox has always been at the center of the human condition. "Man's real life," wrote Carl Jung, "consists of a complex of inexorable opposites—day and night, birth and death, happiness and misery, good and evil. If it were not so, existence would come to an end."

Paradox was a fact of life long before it became a literary and rhetorical device. Who among us has not experienced something ugly in everything beautiful, something true in everything false, something female in something male, or, as King Claudius says in William Shakespeare's *Hamlet,* "mirth in funeral" and "dirge in marriage"? Who among us is not captured by and captured in Alexander Pope's "An Essay on Man"?:

> *Placed on the isthmus of a middle state,*
> *A being darkly wise and rudely great:*
> *With too much knowledge on the Skeptic side,*
> *With too much weakness for the Stoic's pride,*
> *He hangs between; in doubt to act, or rest,*
> *In doubt to deem himself a God, or Beast.*
> *In doubt his mind or body to prefer,*
> *Born but to die, and reasoning but to err;*
>
> . . . .
>
> *Sole judge of Truth, in endless Error hurled:*
> *The glory, jest, and riddle of the world!*

As I—glory, jest, and riddle—finish writing this entry, I suffer a little death. Something has ended, winked out, never to be begun, shaped, or completed again. But, at the same time, as I approach the end, I think of the poet John Donne, who, four centuries ago, chanted the paradoxology of our lives: "Death, thou shalt die."

Now that I'm ending this small disquisition, I'm a bit immortal, too, because I know that you, in another place and another time, are passing your eyes over these words and sharing my thoughts and emotions long after I have struck the symbols on my keyboard, perhaps even after I have slipped this mortal coil.

A Primer of
Political Words

When this book first appears, Americans will be in the grip of a feverish, frenetic, fervent, frantic, and frenzied presidential campaign that demonstrates why in England people stand for election, but in the United States they run. It's also a time that demonstrates although the classical societies of ancient Greece and Rome have vanished, Greek and Roman thought are very much alive in the parlance of politics.

Taking first things first, we'll start with the word *primary*, which descends from the Latin *primus*, "first." *Primary,* as a shortening of "primary election, is first recorded in 1861. In an *election* we "pick out" a candidate whom we wish to vote for. In Latin *e* means "out" and *lectus* "pick or choose."

As the joke goes, the etymology of the word *politics* derives from *poly*, "many," and *tics*, which are bloodsucking parasites. In truth *politics* issues from the Greek word *polities*, "city, citizen." Politics may make strange bedfellows, but, as we shall see, politics makes for even stranger, and sometimes colorful, vocabulary.

Campaign is very much a fighting word. The Latin *campus*, "field," is a clue that the first campaigns were conducted on battlefields. A military campaign is a series of operations mounted to achieve a particular wartime objective. A political campaign is an all-out effort to secure the election of a candidate to office.

When he went to the Forum in Roman times, a candidate for office wore a bleached white toga to symbolize his humility, purity of motive, and candor. The original Latin root, *candidatus*, meant "one who wears white," from the belief that white was the color of purity and probity. There was wishful thinking even in ancient Roman politics, even though a white-clad Roman *candidatus* was accompanied by *sectatores*, followers who helped him get votes by bargaining and bribery. The Latin parent verb *candere*, "to shine, to glow" can be recognized in the English words *candid, candor, candle,* and *incandescent*.

We know that candidates are ambitious; it's also worth knowing that *ambition* developed from the Latin *ambitionem*, "a going about," from the going about of candidates for office in ancient Rome.

President descends from the Latin *praesidio*, "preside, sit in front of or protect." Presidents sit in the seat of government. When we speak of "the ship of state," we are being more accurate etymologically than we know. The Greek word *kybernao* meant "to direct a ship." The Romans borrowed the word as *guberno*, and ultimately it crossed the English Channel as *governor*, originally a steersman. That's why the noun is *governor* and the adjective *gubernatorial*.

The story behind the word *inaugurate* is an intriguing one. It literally means "to take omens from the flight of birds." In ancient Rome, augurs would predict the outcome of an enterprise by the way the birds were flying. These soothsayer-magicians would tell a general whether to march or to do battle by the formations of the birds on the wing. They might even catch one and cut it open to observe its entrails for omens. Nowadays, presidential candidates use their inauguration speeches to take flight on an updraft of words, rather than birds—and they do often spill their guts for all to see.

The original Greek meaning of the word *idiot* was not nearly as harsh as our modern sense. Long before the psychologists got hold of the word, the Greeks used *idiotes*, from the root *idios*, "private," as in *idiom* and *idiosyncrasy*, to designate those who did not hold public office. Because such people possessed no special status or skill, the word *idiot* gradually fell into disrepute.

The vote that we cast is really a "vow" or "wish." And this is the precise meaning of the Latin *votum*. People in our society who fail to exercise their democratic privilege of voting on election day are sometimes called idiots.

A metaphor (the word originally meant "to carry across" in Greek) is a figure of speech that merges two seemingly different objects or ideas. We usually think of metaphors as figurative devices that only poets create, but, in fact, all of us make metaphors during almost every moment of our waking lives. As T. E. Hulme observed, "Prose is a museum, where all the old weapons of poetry are kept."

Take the political expression "to throw one's hat in the ring." The phrase probably derives from the custom of tossing one's hat into the boxing ring to signal the acceptance of a pugilist's challenge. Once the hat is thrown, the candidates start engaging in political infighting as they slug it out with their opponents.

Then there's the idiom "to carry the torch for someone." During the nineteenth century, a dedicated follower showed support for a political candidate by carrying a torch in an evening campaign parade. A fellow who carried a torch in such a rally didn't care who knew that he was wholeheartedly behind his candidate. Later the term was applied to someone publicly (and obsessively) in love.

One more metaphor that was originally literal attaches to bandwagons, high wagons large enough to hold a band of musicians. Early bandwagons were horse-drawn through the streets in order to publicize an upcoming event. Political candidates would ride a bandwagon through a town, and those who wished to show their support would "hop [or climb] on the bandwagon" and ride with the candidate and his blaring band.

Horses and horse racing are dominant animal metaphors that gallop through political life. One of the earliest of equine metaphors is "dark horse." The figure is defined as a political candidate who is nominated unexpectedly, usually as a result of compromise between two factions in a party. Dark-horse candidates who became president include James Polk in 1844, Franklin Pierce in 1852, Rutherford B. Hayes in 1876, James Garfield in 1880, and Warren G. Harding in 1920.

Presidents have running mates. This too is a horse-racing term and derives from the practice of one owner or one stable running two horses in a race, the slower one being put in there to pace the star. The pacesetter was known as the star's running mate. The phrase has been around for more than a century, but its use to define a vice president was coined by, of all non-practitioners of slang, the most scholarly, the most ecclesiastical of presidents, Woodrow Wilson. At the Democratic Convention in 1912 the presidential nomination went to Wilson on the forty-sixth ballot after a terrific brawl. Governor

Wilson of New Jersey announced that his vice presidential choice would be another governor, Thomas Marshall, and announced, "And I feel honored by having him as my running mate." Wilson's turn of phrase brought the house down, the only squeak of humor those assembled had ever heard out of Woodrow Wilson.

The True Meanings
of Christmas

The great English etymologist Owen Barfield once wrote that "words may be made to disgorge the past that is bottled up inside of them, as coal and wine when we kindle or drink them yield up their bottled sunshine." When we uncap the sunshine that is stored inside the many words that relate to the Christmas season, we discover that the light that streams forth illuminates centuries of human history and customs.

The word *Christmas* derives from the Old English *Cristes maesse,* meaning "the festival mass of Christ." *Christmas* is a fine example of a disguised compound, a word formed from two independent morphemes (meaning-bearing elements) that have become so closely welded together that their individual identities have been lost.

Christmas is the only annual religious holiday to have received official and secular sanction by all the states. The word *holiday* itself is another disguised compound, descending from the Old English *haligdaeg,* "holy day." With the change in pronunciation has come a change in meaning so that holidays, such as Independence Day and Labor Day, are not necessarily holy. The *day* morpheme in *holiday* has also transmogrified so that one (especially if one is British) can go "on holiday" for more than one day.

In English-speaking countries, the day following Christmas Day is called Boxing Day. This expression comes from a custom that started in the Middle Ages around eight hundred years ago: Churches would open their alms boxes, in which people had placed gifts of money and distribute the contents to poor people in the neighborhood on the day after Christmas. The tradition continues today; small gifts are often given to couriers such as postal staff and children who deliver newspapers.

The name *Christ* is a translation of the Hebrew word *messiah,* "the anointed one," rendered through the Greek as *Khristos. Jesus* also reaches back to ancient Hebrew and the name Yeshua (Joshua), which is explained as "Jah (or Jahveh, i.e., Jehovah) is salvation."

We learn about Jesus through the *gospels. Gospel* is yet another disguised compound, from the Old English *god,* "good," and *spel,* "news." The four gospels spread the good news of the life and work of Christ. No surprise then that the four men who wrote the gospels are called *evangelists,* from the Greek *euaggelion,* which also means "good news."

The babe was born in *Bethlehem,* a Hebrew word variously interpreted as meaning "house of bread or food," "house of fighting," or "house of the god Lahamut." The Christ child was laid in a *manger,* a word related to the French verb *manger,* "to eat." Why? Because Jesus's crib was a large wooden box that had served as a trough for feeding cattle.

We call the worship of the newborn babe the *Adoration,* from the Latin *adoratio: ad-* "to," *oro-* "pray"; hence, "to pray to." Among those who came to worship were "wise men . . . from the East," *magi,* a Latin word for "magician." Magi were members of an ancient Persian priestly caste of magicians and sorcerers. Incidentally, the number of wise men is never specifically mentioned in the gospels; we infer three from the gifts bestowed on the Christ child.

The letter *X* is the first letter of the word *Xristos,* which in Greek is the word for Christ. *Xmas,* then, is actually a Greek derivative that does not eradicate the name of Christ from *Christmas.* But in reality it is really a legitimate term that was first used within the Greek Orthodox Church.

Yuletide as a synonym for the Christmas season dates back to a pagan and then Christian period of feasting about the time of the winter solstice, December 22. The origin of *yule* is uncertain. One suggestion is that *yule* comes from the Gothic *giul;* or *hiul,* which meant "wheel." In this context, *yule* signifies that the sun, like a wheel, has completed its annual revolution. The Gothic *ol* or *oel* and the Anglo-Saxon *geol,* all meaning "feast," and the Middle English *yollen,* "to cry aloud," have also been considered as sources for *yule.*

Whence the *tide* in *Yuletide?* From an Old English word meaning "time," as in *Eastertide* and "Time and tide wait for no man."

Among the most fascinating Christmas etymologies are those for *Santa Claus* and *Kriss Kringle.* When the Dutch came to the New World, the figure of St. Nicholas, their patron saint, was on the first ship. After the Dutch lost control of New Amsterdam to the English in the seventeenth century, *Sinterklaas* (a form of *St. Nikolaas*) gradually became anglicized into *Santa Claus* and acquired some of the features of the English Father Christmas.

Father Christmas is based on a real person, St. Nicholas. Nicholas was a Christian leader from Myra (in modern-day Turkey) in the 4th century A.D. He was shy and wanted to give money to poor people anonymously. It is said that one day he climbed the roof of a house and dropped a purse of money down the chimney. It landed in a stocking that a girl had put to dry by the fire. This explains the belief that Father Christmas comes down the chimney and places gifts in children's stockings.

Kriss Kringle reflects an even more drastic change from one language to another. The Germans and German-speaking Swiss who settled in Pennsylvania in the early eighteenth century held the custom that the Christ Child, "the Christkindl," brought gifts for the children on Christmas Eve. When these Pennsylvania German (also known as Pennsylvania Dutch) communities were joined by English-speaking settlers, the Christkindl became *Kriss Kringle.* By the 1840s, Kriss Kringle had irretrievably taken on the identity of St. Nicholas, or Santa Claus. Slogans like "Put the Christ back in Christmas" were coined in an effort to remind people of the holiday's origin.

The word *carol* came from a Greek dance called a choraulein, which was accompanied by flute music. The dance later spread throughout Europe and became especially popular with the French, who replaced the flute music with singing. People originally performed carols on several occasions during the year. By the 1600s, carols involved singing only, and Christmas had become the main holiday for these songs.

Most of the carols sung today were originally composed in the 1700s and 1800s. They include "O Little Town of Bethlehem" and "Hark! The Herald Angels Sing." The words of the famous carol "Silent Night" were written on Christmas Eve in 1818 by Joseph Mohr, an Austrian priest. Franz Gruber, the organist of Mohr's church, composed the music that same night, and the carol was sung at midnight Mass. "O Holy Night" was introduced at midnight Mass in 1847. Adolphe Adam, a French composer, wrote the music. Popular nonreligious carols include "Jingle Bells" and "White Christmas."

Of the various plants associated with the Christmas season, the poinsettia possesses the most intriguing history etymologically. A Mexican legend tells of a penniless boy who presented to the Christ Child a beautiful plant with scarlet leaves that resembled the Star of Bethlehem. The Mexicans named the plant *Flor de la Noche Buena,* "Flower of the Holy Night," for Dr. Joel Roberts Poinsett, the first U.S. minister to Mexico, discovered the Christmas flower there in 1828 and brought it to this country, where it was named in his honor in 1836. The poinsettia has become one of the most popular of Christmas plants—and one of the most misspelled and mispronounced *(pointsettia, pointsetta, poinsetta)* words in the English language.

Another botanical Christmas item is the pear tree. In the seasonal song "The Twelve Days of Christmas," have you ever wondered why the true love sends not only a partridge, but an entire pear tree? That's because in the early French version of the song the suitor proffered only a partridge, which in French is rendered as *une pertriz.* A 1718 English version combined the two—"a partridge, une pertriz"—which, slightly corrupted, came out sounding like "a partridge in a pear tree." Through a process known as folk etymology, the partridge has remained proudly perched in a pear tree *(une pertriz)* ever since.

Literature Lives!

Not long ago, a woman telephoned an Atlanta library and asked, "Can you please tell me where Scarlet O'Hara is buried?"

The librarian explained, "Scarlet is a fictional character in Margaret Mitchell's novel *Gone with the Wind*."

"Never mind that," said the caller. "I want to know where she's buried."

For that reader, Scarlet O'Hara had been so alive that she was dead.

Literature lives. Literature endures. Literature prevails. I know this because I know that readers bestow a special kind of life upon people who have existed only in books. Figments though they may be, literary characters can assume a vitality and longevity that pulse more powerfully than flesh and blood. "The strongest memory is weaker than the palest ink," says a Chinese proverb. "A good book is never exhausted. It goes on whispering to you from the wall," Anatole Broyard tells us.

After many years, the publishers of the children's classic *Charlotte's Web* persuaded E. B. White to record his book on tape. So caught had the author become in the web of his arachnid heroine's life that it took nineteen tapings before White could read aloud the passage about Charlotte's death without his voice cracking.

A century earlier, another writer had been deeply affected by the fate of his heroine. Like most of Charles Dickens's works, *The Old Curiosity Shop* (1841) was published in serial form. The novel won a vast readership on both sides of the Atlantic, and as interest in the fate of the heroine, Little Nell, grew intense, circulation reached the staggering figure of one hundred thousand, a record unequaled by any other of Dickens's major novels. In New York, six thousand people crowded the wharf where the ship carrying the final *Master Humphrey's Clock* magazine installment was due to dock. As the vessel approached, the crowd's impatience grew to such a pitch that they cried out as one to the sailors, "Does Little Nell die?"

Alas, Little Nell did die, and tens of thousands of readers' hearts broke. The often ferocious literary critic Lord Jeffrey was found weeping with his head on his library table. "You'll be sorry to hear," he sobbed to a friend, "that little Nelly, Boz's little Nelly, is dead." Daniel O'Connell, an Irish M.P., burst out crying, "He should not have killed her," and then, in anguish, he threw the book out of the window of the train in which he was traveling. A diary of the time records another reader lamenting, "The villain! The rascal! The bloodthirsty scoundrel! He killed my little Nell! He killed my sweet little child!"

That "bloodthirsty scoundrel" was himself shattered by the loss of his heroine. In a letter to a friend Dickens wrote, "I am the wretchedest of the wretched. It [Nell's death] casts the most horrible shadow upon me, and it is as much as I can do to keep moving at all. Nobody will miss her like I shall."

Even more famous than Charlotte and Little Nell is Arthur Conan Doyle's Sherlock Holmes, the world's first consulting detective. The intrepid sleuth's deerstalker hat, Inverness cape, calabash pipe, and magnifying glass are recognized by readers everywhere, and the stories have been translated into more than sixty languages, from Arabic to Yiddish.

Like the heroes of so many popular stories and myths, Sherlock Holmes was born in poverty and nearly died at birth from neglect. Dr. Arthur Conan Doyle was a novice medical practitioner with a dearth of patients. To while away his time and to help pay a few bills, Doyle took pen in hand and created one of the first detectives to base his work squarely on scientific methods.

The publishing world of 1886 did not grasp the revolutionary implications of Doyle's ideas. Editor after editor returned the manuscript with coldly polite rejection notices. After a year and a half, the young author was about to give up hope, when one publisher finally took a chance and bought the rights for five pounds sterling. In December of 1887, Sherlock Holmes came into the world as an unheralded and unnoticed Yuletide child in *Beeton's Christmas Annual*. When, not long after, *The Strand Magazine* began the monthly serialization of the first dozen short stories, entitled *The Adventures of Sherlock Holmes*, the issues sold tens of thousands of copies, and the public furiously clamored for more.

At the height of his success, however, the creator wearied of his creation. He yearned for "higher writing" and felt his special calling to be the historical novel. In December 1893, Doyle introduced into the last story in the Memoirs series the archcriminal Professor James Moriarty. In "The Final Problem," Holmes and the evil professor wrestle at a cliff's edge in Switzerland. Grasping each other frantically, sleuth and villain plummet to their watery deaths at the foot of the Reichenbach Falls.

With Holmes forever destroyed, Doyle felt he could abandon his mystery stories and turn his authorial eyes to the romantic landscapes of the Middle Ages. He longed to chronicle the clangor of medieval battles, the derring-do of brave knights, and the sighs of lovesick maidens. But the writer's tour back in time would not be that easily booked: Sherlock Holmes had taken on a life of his own, something larger than the will of his creator. The normally staid, stiff-upper-lipped British public was first bereaved, then outraged. Conservative London stockbrokers went to work wearing black armbands in mourning for the loss of their heroic detective. Citizens poured out torrents of letters to editors complaining of Holmes's fate. One woman picketed Doyle's home with a sign branding him a murderer.

The appeals of *The Strand*'s publishers to Doyle's sensibilities and purse went unheeded. For the next eight years Holmes lay dead at the bottom of the Swiss falls while Doyle branched out into historical fiction, science fiction, horror stories, and medical stories. But he wasn't very good at "higher writing."

Finally, Doyle could resist the pressures from publisher and public no more. He wrote what may be the best of all the Holmes stories, "The Hound of the Baskervilles," which was immediately serialized in *The Strand*. As the story made clear, Holmes had not returned from his demise as reported in 1893. This tale was merely a reminiscence, set in 1888. Still, the reappearance of Sherlock Holmes fired the public imagination and enthusiasm; readers again queued up by the thousands to buy the monthly installments of the magazine. In 1903, ten years after his "death," Doyle's detective rose up from his watery grave in the Reichenbach Falls, his logical wonders to perform for the whole world.

The Return of Sherlock Holmes, the series of thirteen stories that brought back Doyle's hero, was greeted eagerly by patient British readers whose appetites had been whetted by "Hound," and the author continued writing stories of his detective right into 1927. When, in 1930, Arthur Conan Doyle died at age seventy-one, readers around the world mourned his passing. Newspaper cartoons portraying a grieving Sherlock Holmes captured the public's sense of irreparable loss.

Such is the power of mythic literature that the creation has outlived his creator. Letters and packages from all over the world still come addressed to "Sherlock Holmes" at 221-B Baker Street, now home to the Sherlock Holmes Museum. Only Santa Claus gets more mail, at least just before Christmastime. More movies—well over three hundred of them—have been made about Holmes than about Dracula, Frankenstein, Robin Hood, and Rocky combined. Sherlock Holmes stories written by post-Doylean authors now vastly outnumber the sixty that Doyle produced. More than 150 societies in homage to Sherlock Holmes are active in the United States alone.

However many times the progenitor tried to finish off his hero, by murder or retirement or flat refusal to write any more adventures, the Great Detective lives, vigilant and deductive as ever, protecting the humble from the evils that lurk in the very heart of our so-called civilization. Despite his "death" more than a hundred years ago, Sherlock Holmes has never died. Readers around the world simply won't let him.

Benjamin Franklin was a guest at a Paris dinner party when a question was posed: What condition of man most deserves pity? Each guest proposed an example of a miserable situation. When Franklin's turn came, he responded, "A lonesome man on a rainy day who does not know how to read." Because you are still reading this book (in one form or another), you must be a bibliophile. As a member of that happy and privileged band, you will never be lonely. You enjoy the company and conversation of thousands of men and women, ancient and contemporary, learned and entertaining, who have set their humanity to paper and crafted language into literature.

IT'S A
PUNDERFUL LIFE

Jest for the Pun of It

E arly in 1989, I received a delicious invitation: "The International Save the Pun Foundation cordially invites you to the Fourth Annual Punsters Dinner at Mareva's Restaurant in Chicago. Special guest speaker John Crosbie, Founder and Cheerman of the Bored, and Punster of the Year, Richard Lederer. Come pun, come all!"

Accompanying the invitation was a map of "Oh Pun Territory," marked by such features as *Lord's Prairie, Forever Moor, Joan Rivers, Gerald and Henry Fjord, Sit-Up-Strait, Lloyd Bridges, Piggy Bank, Oh-Say-Can-You-Sea, Sexual Peak, Dis-a-Point, Psycho Path, Woody Allen, Gene Autree, W. C. Fields, Air-Plain,* and *George Bush.* The date of the dinner was April Fool's Day, of course.

Yes, Virginia, there really is an International Save the Pun Foundation (ISPF), a verbal glee club dedicated to wordy causes like preserving the pun as an endangered specious. At the end of 1988 had come a letter from John Crosbie, the presiding gray eminence of the Pun Foundation. Mr. Crosbie's message began, "We are delighted to confirm that this Foundation has chosen you to receive its International Punster of the Year Award for 1989, based on your latest book, *Get Thee to a Punnery.*" Thrilled to be designated as Attila the Pun, the top pun and fastest punslinger of the Western world, I immediately sent off a reply that started with this salutation—

—a rebus that translates into "Dear John Crosbie." You'll get the idea of the whole letter from its first paragraph: "I am all charged up and positively ec-static about the electrifying news that you are planning to socket to me and plugging me to go on the circuit as your Punster of the Year. To re-fuse such a creative outlet would be re-volting to the point of battery. In short, I am de-lighted."

I know. You're a groan up who thinks that I'm a compulsive puntificator cursed with a pukish, not puckish, imagination. You suspect, I suspect, that I'm a member of the Witless Protection Program. That's all right with me because I amused to wit and always bear in mind the slogan of the International Save the Pun Foundation: "A day without puns is a day without sunshine. There is gloom for improvement."

For all of us who have experienced the loneliness of the long-distance punner, the dinner in Chicago was the farce that launched a thousand quips. More than two hundred loaded punslingers attended, pleased to have so many pun pals to go out wit.

Punnery is largely the trick of compacting two or more ideas within a single word or expression. Punnery challenges us to apply the greatest pressure per square syllable of language. Punnery surprises us by flouting the law of nature that pretends that two things cannot occupy the same space at the same time. Punnery is an exercise of the mind at being concise.

Punning is a rewording experience. The inveterate (not invertebrate) punster believes that a good pun is like a good steak—a rare medium well done. In such a prey on words, *rare, medium,* and *well done* are double entendres, so that six meanings are crammed into the space ordinarily occupied by just three.

The pun is mightier than the sword, and often sharper—and at the International Save the Pun Foundation festivities, one was much more likely to run into a pun than a sword, as everybody present took a blue ribbin'. The hours fled away because, as one frog said to the other, "Time's fun when you're having flies!" Put that one in your funny pile—and your punny file.

The highlight of the evening was the appearance of the pun made flesh in the person of Joyce Heitler, the president of the Chicago Chapter of the ISPF, who each year comes dressed as the "Pun-Up Girl," attired in visual puns that the audience had to decipher.

On her head Joyce wore a small weaving mechanism, translating to *frame of mind* or *hair loom*. Her dress was splashed with dots and dashes—*dress code*. On her finger Joyce wore a ring woven out of red hair—*red hair ring*. Around her neck was a lace collar. An easy one: *neck-lace*.

Joyce's most enticing sartorial challenge was that she claimed to be wearing a visual oxymoron—an outward and visible sign of two opposite ideas, such as *jumbo shrimp, pretty ugly*, or *old news*. I spotted an airless inner tube slung over Joyce's shoulder and under her arm. "Flat busted!" I shouted, confident that I had identified the hidden oxymoron. "No, you silly," replied Joyce. "This is at-tire, or, if you wish, a boob tube," at which point this stud re-tired from the competition treading lightly. The oxymoronic solution reposed in the *loose tights* that Joyce was sporting.

Among the evening's delights was a "Rap-Pun Contest" (someone suggested "Rap-Pun-Sel") in which each table of pundits composed a string of puns to rap rhythms. One of the best raps included these verses of poetree. Try reading it aloud rap-aciously:

> *"Oh, Juniper, grow by my side."*
> *The Oak bent down to plant a kiss.*
> *"Someday we will exchange our boughs*
> *And live our lives in wooded bliss."*
>
> *Then Juniper axed her lover Oak*
> *In the morning forest dew,*
> *"Willow bend your limbs abought me,*
> *Maple I wood pine fir yew."*

As Francis Bacon once almost said, without hamming it up, some puns are to be tasted, others to be swallowed, and a few to be chewed and digested. Mareva's is living proof and reproof that a Polish gourmet restaurant is not an oxymoron, and, even though Joyce Heitler proclaimed, "We don't serve soup to nuts," a delicious borscht was brought out, inspiring one punhead to call out, "The heartbeet of America!" The foundation initially thought about holding the dinner in a new restaurant on the moon, a perfect place for a bunch of lunatics. But an investigation revealed that while the Moonie restaurant has great food, it doesn't have any atmosphere.

Then, just for the halibut, the international punsters took a Pole and came up with a number of fishy suggestions for an ideal punsters' menu, a buffet of sole food. Among the tour de farces highest on the scales of effishiency were *salmon rushdie, tuna turner, poisson ivy, bass ackwards, dill pickerel, brain sturgeon, combination lox, porgy best, turn pike,* and *win one for the kipper.* That night the world was our roister. And did you know that a noise annoys an oys-ter?

If you are one to carp about these finny lines, you must be hard of herring.

Pun Your Way
to Success

Many luminaries have proffered punderful advice on how to succeed in the business of life and the life of business. "Don't be a carbon copy of someone else. Make your own impression," punned French philosopher Voltaire. "Even if you're on the right track, you'll get run over if you just sit there," advised humorist Will Rogers centuries later.

Sharpen your pun cells, and get right to wit:

- The only place where success comes before work is in the dictionary.
- The difference between a champ and a chump is *u*.
- Triumph is just *umph* added to *try*.
- Don't assume. It will make an *ass* out of *u* and *me*.
- Hard work is the yeast that raises the dough.
- The best vitamin for making friends is B-1.
- Break a bad habit—drop it.
- Patience is counting down without blasting off.
- Patience requires a lot of wait.
- Minds are like parachutes: they function only when open.
- To keep your mind clean and healthy, change it every once in a while.
- You can have an open mind without having a hole in your head.
- Of all the things you wear, your expression is the most important.
- If at first you don't succeed, try, try a grin.

"Big shots are only little shots that keep on shooting," observed British writer Christopher Morley. Here are some more punderful maxims that merit a blue ribbin':

- One thing you can give and still keep is your word.
- A diamond is a chunk of coal that made good under pressure.
- When the going gets tough, the tough get going.
- If the going gets easy, you may be going downhill.
- If you must cry over spilled milk, please try to condense it.
- Don't be afraid to go out on a limb, that's where the fruit is.
- Read the Bible—it will scare the hell out of you.
- The Ten Commandments are not multiple choice.
- Failure is the path of least persistence.
- Life is not so much a matter of position as disposition.

"Many people would sooner die than think—and usually they do," lamented British philosopher Bertrand Russell, pun in cheek. Some puns can help us to climb the ladder of success without getting rung out:

- People who never make a mistake never make anything else.
- When you feel yourself turning green with envy, you're ripe to be plucked.
- A smile doesn't cost a cent, but it gains a lot of interest.
- Success is more attitude than aptitude.
- Having a sharp tongue can cut your own throat.
- Learn that the bitter can lead to the better.
- He who throws mud loses ground.
- Hug your kids at home, but belt them in a car.
- Fear is the darkroom where negatives are developed.
- Humans are like steel. When they lose their tempers, they are worthless.
- Don't learn safety rules by accident. Don't be dead to rites.
- There are two finishes for automobiles—lacquer and liquor.
- Learn from the nail. Its head keeps it from going too far.
- He who laughs, lasts.

Even though it's a jungle out there, a real zoo, this collection of beastly puns may help you succeed in a workaday world that depends on survival of the fittest:

- Be like a turtle. You'll make progress by coming out of your shell and sticking your neck out.

- Speaking of sticking your neck out, be like a giraffe. Reach higher than all the others, and you'll have the best perspective on life. You'll be head and shoulders above the general herd, and everybody will then look up to you.

- Be like the birds. They have bills, too, but they keep on singing.

- Be like a duck. Keep calm and unruffled on the surface, but paddle like crazy underneath.

- Be like a beaver. Don't get stumped. Just cut things down to size and build one dammed thing after another for the future.

- Be like a cat. Claw your way to the top. That's what drapes are for.

- Be like a dog. Be loyal. Enjoy the wind in your face. Run barefoot, romp, and play daily. Leave yourself breathless at least once a day. Chase your tail in an effort to make ends meet. And be sure to leave your mark on the world.

- Be like a chicken. Act like a smart cluck, rule the roost, and suck seed.

- Be like a horse. Use some horse sense and stable thinking and be able to say "nay."

- Be like an owl. Look all around, be wise, and give a hoot.

- Be like a lion. Live life with pride and grab the lion's share with might and mane.

- Be like a rhino. Be thick-skinned and charge ahead to make your point.

- Be like an oyster. It takes a lot of grit to make a pearl of great value.

- Be like a sponge. Soak up everything, and be helpful in the kitchen.

- Be like a spider. Surf the web and pull all the right strings.

- Be like a squirrel. Go out on a limb to prepare for hard times.

- Be like a kangaroo. Advance through life by leaps and bounds, and keep your family close to you.

- Be like a frog. Be comfortable on land and water—and if something bugs you, snap it up.

- Be like a mole. You know you're living on burrowed time, so stay down-to-earth and well-grounded. Forge ahead by digging as deep as you can.

- Be like a flamingo. Don't be afraid of looking odd, as long as you have a leg to stand on.

- Be like an eagle. Travel in the highest circles, stay eagle-eyed, and swoop down on every opportunity.

- Be like the woodpecker. Just keep pecking away until you finish the job. You'll succeed by using your head and proving that opportunity knocks more than once.

- Don't be like a lemming. Avoid following the crowd and jumping to conclusions.

- And remember that the only things you find in the middle of the road are yellow stripes and dead armadillos.

Nothing Works for Me

Some people hold the same job for their entire career. Others move from one job to another while relentlessly ascending the corporate ladder. My personal workplace history is more checkered, so I'll make a game of it:

- My first job was working in an orange juice factory, but I couldn't concentrate on the same old boring rind, so I got canned.
- Then I became a lumberjack, but I just couldn't hack it, so they gave me the axe.
- I was next employed at a diet center, but I got downsized.
- I became a baker, but I turned out to be a loafer and couldn't make enough dough.
- Then I opened a donut shop, but I soon got tired of the hole business.
- I manufactured calendars, but my days were numbered.
- After that I tried to be a tailor, but I just wasn't suited for it. Mainly because it was a sew-sew job, de-pleting and de-pressing.
- I took a job as an upholsterer, but I never recovered.
- Next I worked in a muffler factory, but that was exhausting.
- I became a drill press operator, but the job was too boring.
- I wanted to be a barber, but I just couldn't cut it.
- I became a hairdresser, but the job was just too cut-and-dried.
- I tried telemarketing, but I had too many hang-ups.
- I manned a computer but developed a terminal illness and lost my drive and my memory.
- I sold origami, but the business folded.

- I became a judge, but the job was too trying and soon lost its appeal.
- Then I tried to be a chef. I figured it would add a little spice to my life, but I just didn't have the thyme.
- I attempted to be a deli worker, but any way I sliced it, I couldn't cut the mustard.
- I enjoyed being a professional musician, but eventually I found I wasn't noteworthy. I just didn't know my brass from my oboe.
- I studied a long time to become a doctor, but I didn't have any patients.
- I took a job at UPS, but I couldn't express myself.
- Next was a job in a shoe factory, but the job didn't last and I got the boot.
- I became a Velcro salesman, but couldn't stick with it.
- I was a professional fisherman but discovered that I couldn't live on my net income.
- I thought about becoming a witch, so I tried that for a spell.
- I was a masseur for a while, but I rubbed people the wrong way.
- I became a Hawaiian garland maker, but I got leid off.
- So I turned to designing lingerie, but I got the pink slip.
- I tried being a fireman, but I suffered burnout.
- I became a banker, but I lacked interest and maturity and finally withdrew from the job.
- I managed to get a good job working for a pool maintenance company, but the work was just too draining.
- I got a job at a zoo feeding giraffes, but I was fired because I wasn't up to it.
- So then I became a personal trainer in a gym, but they said I wasn't fit for the job.
- I tried selling cigarette lighters, but I lost my spark.
- Next, I found being an electrician interesting, but found the work shocking and revolting, so they discharged me.
- I got a job as a historian until I realized there was no future in it.
- I became a cardiologist, but my heart just wasn't in it.

- I became a tennis pro, but it wasn't my racket. I was too high strung.
- I tried being a teacher, but I soon lost my principal, my faculties, and my class.
- I trained to be a ballet dancer, but it was too-too difficult.
- I tried being a farmer, but I wasn't outstanding in my field.
- Then I was a pilot, but I didn't have the right altitude.
- I was also a Viagra salesman, but I couldn't keep it up.
- I worked at Starbucks, but I had to quit because it was always the same old grind.
- I became a statistician, but I got broken down by age, sex, and marital status.
- Finally, I was a Scrabble champion, but I became inconsonant, and I can't move my vowels anymore.

So I've retired, and I find I'm a perfect fit for this job!

A Bilingual Pun
Is Twice the Fun

A good pun is its own reword, and bilingual puns are twice as rewording as those that stay within the boundaries of a single language. Some of the most pyrotechnic puns have a French twist, into which you can sink your teeth—*bon mot*lars, perhaps:

- Why do the French need only one egg to make an omelet? Because in France, one egg is *un oeuf*.

- Have you stayed at the new luxury hotel in town? It's a site for soirees.

- Have you heard about the student in Paris who spent too much time sitting in a hard chair studying? She got sore buns.

- Have you heard about the milkmaid who worked on a really big farm? She had a prominent dairy air.

- A company tried to manufacture prosthetic devices for feline amputees, but found there was no market for the product. You might say that they committed a faux paw.

- Knock, knock. Who's there ? Comet Halley. Comet Halley who? Tres bien, merci. Et vous?

- A feline kept yakking away inappropriately. Finally, his fellow felines tied an anchor around his legs and threw him in to a river. The result: undue twaddle; cat sank.

- "I hate reading Victor Hugo," said Les miserably.

- Motto of the three musketeers: "En garde, we thrust."

- A class of second graders inadvertently came up with a French pun. After an especially hard day, the teacher sighed aloud, "C'est la vie."

  With one voice the children called out, "La vie!"

- A snail oozed into an automobile showroom, pulled out $50,000 in crisp bills and ordered a fancy red convertible. "One favor," the snail requested. "Please paint a big *S* on each of the doors."

  "Sure," said the salesman, "but why would you want that?"

  The snail replied: "So that when my friends see me driving down the street, they can all shout, 'Look at the *S* car go!'"

Great bilingual tropes brighten languages other than French. The all-time prize for transmitting the fullest message with the greatest compactness must go to Sir Charles James Napier. In 1843, Napier quelled an uprising in the Indian province of Sind and announced his triumph via telegram to his commanders in London. All he wrote was the one word *Peccavi*.

The Foreign Office broke into cheers. In an age when all gentlemen studied Latin, Napier never doubted that his superiors would remember the first-person past perfect tense of *peccare*—and would properly translate his message as "I have sinned."

Here are some polyglot plays on words that should be understandable, even without much knowledge of a second language:

- At an Italian restaurant I don't know whether I'm antipasto or provolone.

- Have you heard about the liberated Irish woman? Her name was Erin Go Braless.

- And have you met these famous Irish men and women?: the Irish botanist Phil O'Dendren, the Irish theater owner Nick O'Lodeon, the Irish cigarette manufacturer Nick O'Teen, the Irish marksman Rick O'Shay, the Irish meteorologist Barry O'Metric, the Irish printer Mimi O'Graph, the Irish playwright Mel O'Drama, the Irish poet Ann O'Nymous, the Irish singers Mary O'Lanza and Carrie O'Key, and the Irish designer for outdoor living Patty O'Furniture.

- When a pig roast takes place in England, several boars are needed to feed the hungry, but in Russia, one Boris Gudonov.

- Have you heard about the Chinese restaurant that stays open twenty-four hours a day? It's called Wok Around the Clock.
- Have you visited the Jewish section of India's capital city? It's called Kosher Delhi.
- Does that last pun get a standing oy vaytion?
- No question about it. Adolf Hitler created a terrible fuehrer.
- What do you call a secondhand clothing store in India? Whose Sari Now?
- When Brutus told Julius Caesar that he had eaten a whole squab, Caesar replied, "Et tu, Bruté."
- A classics teacher in Maine owns a boat that he's christened *Navego,* which is Latin for "I sail" and pronounced "Now we go."
- Mexican weather report: Chili today, hot tamale.
- A Mexican visiting the United States went into a store to buy a pair of socks. He spoke no English, and the clerk didn't know a word of Spanish. Through pantomime, the Mexican tried to explain what he needed, without much success. The clerk brought out shoes, then tried sneakers, then slippers, then laces—all to no avail.

  Finally, he came out of the stockroom with a pair of socks, and the Mexican exclaimed, "Eso sí que es!"

  Exclaimed the exasperated clerk, "Well, for crying out loud. If you could spell it, why didn't you say so in the first place?"
- There are many stories related to the sinking of the Titanic. Some have just come to light owing to the success of the movie. For example, most people don't know that back in 1912, Hellmann's mayonnaise was manufactured in England. The Titanic was carrying twelve thousand jars of the condiment scheduled for delivery in Vera Cruz, Mexico, which was to be the next port of call for the great ship after New York City.

  The Mexican people were eagerly awaiting delivery and were disconsolate at the loss. So much so that they declared a national day of mourning which they still observe today.

  It is known, of course, as Sinko de Mayo.

- On a Monday morning, the mayor of New York gathered reporters and announced the rejuvenation of the ailing New York City transit system. The *New York Daily News* reporter covering the story realized that the situation was too good to be true. His headline read: SICK TRANSIT'S GLORIOUS MONDAY.

- Chico Marx once took umbrage upon hearing someone exultantly exclaim, "Eureka!"

  Chagrined, Chico shot back, "You doan smella so good yourself!"

My Favorite Monsters

Three vampires went into a bar and sat down. A buxom barmaid came over to take their orders. The vampires tried to be neck romancers, so they batted their eyes and flirted with her by telling her how much they liked her blood type. But she rebuffed them with the reply "O negative" and asked, "And what would you, er, gentlemen like tonight?"

The first vampire said, "I'll have a mug of blood."

The second vampire said, "I'll have a mug of blood."

The third vampire shook his head at his companions and said, "I'll have a glass of plasma."

The barmaid called out to the bartender, "Two bloods and a blood light!"

Then they all toasted each other by shouting, "This blood's for you!"

Vampires love to drink blood because they find it thicker than water. In fact, we know a vampire who was fired as night watchman at a blood bank. They caught him drinking on the job, thus making too many unauthorized withdrawals. And he took too many coffin breaks.

Long ago vampires sailed to the United States in blood vessels and set up their own terror-tories. Many of them settled in the Vampire State, and others went west and became batboys for the Colorado Rockies' Horror Picture Show. Some went on to college and earned a place in Phi Batta Cape-a. Others perfected their skills at sucking blood by attending law school.

Vampires from all over the world gather each fall deep in the forests of Transylvania to renew their commitment to their calling. They reverently view the scroll, written and signed in blood, that contains

151

their history and lists their rites and responsibilities. Then, at midnight, they stand at attention and swear allegiance to the Draculation of Vein Dependence.

The most famous of all vampires is, of course, Count Dracula, the notorious neck-rophiliac. He can be a real pain in the neck, but he can get under your skin. Even if he pays for dinner, he'll still put the bite on you.

Dracula once fell in love at first fright with the girl necks door. She was six feet tall, and Dracula loves to suck up to women. But he's remained a bat-chelor his whole life because anytime he courts another vampire, they end up at each other's throats. Or he finds out that his sweetie just isn't his blood type.

And any mortal woman to whom Dracula is attracted soon realizes that life with him will be an unfailingly draining experience, so she's not likely to stick her neck out for him. It's hard to get a good night's sleep with him because of the terrible coffin.

Moreover, Dracula isn't a very attractive fellow, in large part because he can't see himself in the bat-room mirror and is thus unable to brush his teeth, comb his hair, or tie his tie. This causes bat breath and the disease Dracula fears most—tooth decay. The fiend went to the dentist to correct his bite, but he still ended up with false teeth, which for him are new-fangled devices that, like Dracula himself, come out at night.

Dracula finds his victims in any neck of the woods and as he sucks their blood, he sings, "You're So Vein" and "Fangs for the Mammaries!" Whenever the police come after him, the count simply explains that he is a law-a-biting citizen. He loves the deep plots and grave setting of a cemetery, especially when the temperature rises above 90 degrees. Dracula often sighs, "There's nothing like a cold bier and a bloody Mary on a hot day." Sometimes Dracula has to wait interminably to emerge from his coffin. To him it seems that the sun never sets on the brutish vampire.

Halloween is a time when we conjure up visions of all manner of ghoulies and ghosties and long-leggety beasties. Along with Dracula, the most popular of these grotesques is the Frankenstein monster, not to be confused with Victor Frankenstein, his creator.

Despite his evil reputation, Dr. Victor Frankenstein actually had a good sense of humor—he kept his monster in stitches. Frankenstein was also a philanthropist because he founded the first organ donor program—a dead giveaway to his good heart. He also loved his dog—a black Lab, of course. And when the monster rose from the table and spat on the ground, the proud doctor exclaimed, "It's saliva! It's saliva!"

Doctor Frankenstein's assistant, Igor, was also a doctor and together they were a pair o' docs. When they decided to stop making monsters, Igor found a new job at an auto dealership as parts manager.

Even though Frankenstein's monster's twisted body strikes us as shocking and re-volting, he had his heart in the right place. In fact, he once had a ghoul friend to take out for a frank 'n' stein. He just couldn't resistor. Now he has a new ghoul friend named Endora. He'd previously dated a lady scarecrow but went from rags to witches.

Sensitive fellow that old Zipperneck was, he also developed an identity crisis. He kept hoping that he had a mummy and dead-y, but they never appeared. So he went to a psychiatrist to see if he had a screw loose. One day he decided to take the five o'clock train. But the authorities made him give it back. Actually, the townspeople came to love Frankenstein's monster; they carried a torch for him.

Ultimately, the government re-monster-ated Doctor Frankenstein and sued for custody of his amazing creation. Since both parties demanded sole custody in the Frankenstein lawsuit, the judge called for a sword-of-Solomon socket wrench and ruled an equitable split: the government was granted permission to raise the creature's grotesque body, while Victor reared its ugly head.

Almost as central in our popular culture is the image of the werewolf. Did you know that werewolves love to eat sheep because they can dine and floss at the same time?

One day a fellow went to a clinic and complained, "Doctor, doctor! I feel like I'm a werewolf." The doctor replied, "Have a seat and comb your face."

Wolfman lived in San Francisco. When he felt mischievous, he would moon at the bay. Afterwards, he moved to a larger community of werewolves—Howlywood—where he auditioned for bit parts.

His vulpine body caused him to soil his clothes frequently, so he had to visit the Laundromat almost every day. He became a washin' werewolf. He also took up clay-spinning as a hobby and became a hairy potter.

ANSWERS TO GAMES
AND QUIZZES

A Guide to Britspeak, A to Zed (page 11)

1. billion - a million million in Britain, a thousand million in the U. S., biscuit - cracker or cookie, bitter - beer, bob - one shilling, or a small amount of money, braces - suspenders, catapult - slingshot, chemist - druggist, chips - French fried potatoes, crisp - potato chip, dinner jacket - tuxedo, full stop - period, ground floor - first floor, hockey - ice hockey, ice - ice cream, jelly - gelatin dessert, knickers - women's underpants, lift - elevator, M.P. - Member of Parliament, minister - cabinet member, plaster - Band-Aid, pocketbook - pocket notebook or billfold, public school - private school, pudding - dessert, spectacles - eye glasses, stone - fourteen lbs., stuff - unprintable in this respectable book, sweet - dessert, till - cash register, tin - can, torch - flashlight, vest -undershirt, waistcoat - vest

2. aisle - gangway, bar - pub, bathroom - loo or W.C. (water closet), bobby pin - hair grip, clothes pin - clothes-peg, counterclockwise - anti-clockwise, hardware store - ironmonger, intermission – interval, kerosene - paraffin, napkin - serviette, quilt -eiderdown, shrimp - prawn, sled - sledge, silverware - cutlery, swimsuit - swim costume, telephone booth - call booth or kiosk, thumb tack - drawing pin or push-pin, the letter *z* - zed

3. advert - advertisement, banger - sausage, bobby - policeman, chucker-out - bouncer, don - college teacher, draughts - checkers, dressing gown -bathrobe, dustbin - trash can, fortnight - two weeks, hoover - vacuum cleaner, plimsolls - sneakers, porridge -oatmeal, pram - baby carriage, scone - baking-powder biscuit, spanner - wrench, starter - appetizer, switchback - roller coaster, takeaway - take-out, telly - television

4. ett, bean, bown, clark, dyutee, eyethur, eevohlushun, feah, figger, GArage, herb (with the *h* sounded), labORatory (five syllables), lezhur, leftenant, missyle, pahtriot, prihvacee (short *i*), shedule, SECretry (three syllables), sujjest, tomahto (but potayto), vihtamin (short *i*), zehbra

5. aeroplane, aluminium, cheque, defence, fibre, grey, inflexion, enquire, gaol, jewellery, judgement, manoeuvre, marvellous, organisation, pyjamas, plough, programme, speciality, spelt, storey, tonnes, phial, whisky

6. China are leading the world in exports, different to, in hospital, living in Baker Street.

Under a Spell (page 56)

All the words in the list are spelled correctly. If you just happened to circle some of the words, compare your vision of each circled word with each given spelling. This will help you to conquer your personal spelling demons.

Fairly Familiar Phrases (page 65)

1. aweigh 2. bated 3. bear 4. bite 5. bloc 6. seeded 7. champing or chomping 8. complement 9. chord 10. deserts

11. faze 12. flair 13. foul 14. hale/hearty 15. hair's breadth 16. whole 17. indeed 18. jibe 19. lam 20. manner born

21. martial 22. mettle 23. might/main 24. pale 25. pique 26. pie 27. pidgin 28. plane 29. pore 30. praying

31. principle 32. rack 33. rein 34. raise Cain 35. rapt 36. reckless 37. wreak 38. rite 39. shoo- 40. sic

41. sleight 42. spitting 43. stamping 44. stanch 45. straits 46. tow 47. toe 48. trouper 49. vain 50. whet

Words That Never Stray (page 92)

1. taken aback 2. far afield 3. malice aforethought 4.self aggrandizing 5. arms akimbo 6. run amok 7. in arrears 8. artesian well 9. look askance 10. go astray

11. under the auspices of 12. anchors aweigh 13. go awry 14. bald-faced/barefaced lie 15. at one's behest 16. on bended knee 17. bide one's time 18. blithering idiot 19. bogged down 20. take a breather

21. breakneck speed 22. briny deep 23. country bumpkin 24. busman's holiday 25. Let bygones be bygones 26.in cahoots 27. champing at the bit 28. dandle on one's knee 29. by dint of 30. dipsy doodle

31. knock-down drag-out 32. if I had my druthers 33. high dudgeon 34. eke out 35.extenuating circumstances 36. figment of the imagination 37. fine-tooth come 38. foregone conclusion 39. Heaven forfend 40. on the fritz

41. gainful employment 42. old geezer 43. gibbous moon 44. gird one's loins 45. grist for the mill 46. gung ho 47. all gussied up 48. halcyon days 49. go haywire 50. ward heeler

51. time immemorial 52. make inroads 53. well intentioned 46. keeled over 55. put the kibosh on 56. coffee klatch 57. on the lam 58. lickety split 59. in lieu of 60. at loggerheads

61. the madding crowd 62. fair to middling 63. misspent youth 64. high muckamuck 65. neap tide 66. noised abroad 67.whisper sweet nothings 68. to the nth degree 69. in the offing 70. opposable thumb

71. hoist with one's own petard 72. peter out 73. pinking shears 74. Pyrrhic victory 75. raring to go 76. good riddance 77. ride rough-shod 78. rumpus room 79. runcible spoon 80. inner sanctum

81. scot-free 82. the scruff of the neck 83. self-fulfilling prophecy 84. the whole shebang 85. shored up 86. sleight of hand 87. suborn perjury 88. moral suasion 89.tit for tat 90. (s)he went thataway

91. in the throes of 92. toed the line 93. in a tizzy 94. in a trice 95. treasure trove 96. moral turpitude 97. ulterior motive 98. take umbrage 99. unsung hero 100. vale of tears

101. vantage point 102. wend one's way 103. whiled away the time 104. young whippersnapper 105. wishful thinking 106. as is one's wont 107. workaday world 108. wax wroth 109. days of yore 110. zoot suit

111. aid and abet 112. alas and alack 113. the be-all and end-all 114. beck and call 115. betwixt and between 116. kit and caboodle 117. dribs and drabs 118. to and fro 119. hale and hearty 120. hem and haw

121. for all intents and purposes 122. kith and kin 123. null and void 124. pomp and circumstance 125. spick and span 126. hither and thither 127. trials and tribulations 128. vim and vigor 129. whys and wherefores 130. hither and yon